D1505508

THE NATURAL ORDER OF MONEY

The Natural Order of Money

ROY SEBAG

Chelsea Green Publishing
White River Junction, Vermont
London, UK

Copyright © 2022 by Roy Sebag.
All rights reserved.

No part of this book may be transmitted or reproduced
in any form by any means without permission
in writing from the publisher.

Originally published in the United Kingdom
in 2022 by Goldmoney Publishing.
This edition published by Chelsea Green Publishing, 2023.

Printed in the United States of America.
First printing April 2023.
10 9 8 7 6 5 4 3 2 1   23 24 25 26 27

ISBN 978-1-91529-422-7

Our Commitment to Green Publishing
Chelsea Green sees publishing as a tool for cultural change and ecological stewardship. We strive to align our book manufacturing practices with our editorial mission and to reduce the impact of our business enterprise in the environment. We print our books and catalogs on chlorine-free recycled paper, using vegetable-based inks whenever possible. This book may cost slightly more because it was printed on paper that contains recycled fiber, and we hope you'll agree that it's worth it. *The Natural Order of Money* was printed on paper supplied by Sheridan that is made of recycled materials and other controlled sources.

Chelsea Green Publishing
White River Junction, Vermont, USA
London, UK

www.chelseagreen.com

CONTENTS

Author's Preface   ix

THE NATURAL ORDER OF MONEY

I

What makes cooperation possible and sustainable between people and the natural world?—We must turn to the natural order—Modern economic theory deals with analysis in a mathematical vacuum, removed from its wider ecological environment—This work is an exercise in natural philosophy that is occupied with the synthesis of the living, breathing economy.   1

II

Time is the fundamental, superseding law of nature—Time moves forward and is irreversible—Human action is beholden to the requirements of the present—Contemporary economics tends to ignore the condition of our temporality—The essential features of nature emerge within the omnipresent theatre of time.   5

III

Nature is a thermodynamic system governed by the forces of energy and entropy—Metabolization is the process of conserving and expending energy—Energy sources which propel this thermodynamic system are foods, fuels, and elemental substances. 9

IV

The human cooperative system is also thermodynamic— There is a chain of temporal energy dependency, in which the first cause of an economy is those who work with nature to source foods, fuels, and elemental substances— The real economy generates energy embodiments; the service economy only consumes them—The perfect cycle of the farmer's activity—The real economy is beholden to a natural standard of measure and reward. 15

V

Ecological accountability is a fact of nature and of all human cooperative systems—Only the service economy is able to artificially and temporarily ignore ecological accountability—When ecological accountability is manipulated or forgotten, the relationship between the real and service economies becomes parasitic—The natural standard must be reified and extended to all members ensuring that ecological accountability remains at the heart of cooperation. 25

VI

Ecological accountability is not an ideal or promise, but a lived reality—Money extends the natural standard, promoting cooperation while reflecting ecological accountability—Money itself must be an energy embodiment—Money is more than its incidental features—This understanding of money differs from standard accounts in modern economic and anthropological theory. 31

VII

A superior money will be resistant to entropy and rare or difficult to extract from nature—True money will neither be food nor fuel, but rather an elemental substance—Elements are naturally scarce, meaning that each element exhibits certain unchanging qualities—Gold is the apex element within the natural order of money. 39

VIII

When money is gold, cooperation between people and nature is sustainable—Gold money remains a stable measure and reward in both generative and degenerative cycles—We live in an age of contrived moneys and parasitic economies—A solution must be given by nature and not the service economy—Gold is the perfect mirror of ecological accountability. 49

Appendix I   57
Appendix II   63
Notes   77
Index   85

PREFACE

The thoughts which follow are the product of my own philosophical investigations into the nature of human cooperation and money over a period of 18 years. During those years, I enjoyed a successful career as an entrepreneur, having founded businesses engaged in the farming, mining, investment management, technology, and manufacturing industries.

I began writing some of these ideas down nearly a decade ago with the intent to publish them as a book. This was to be a very different kind of book, one that was voluminous and highly technical. The first manuscript, completed in 2018, was nearly ten times the size of the current one. But something about the process of publishing that book felt inauthentic to me and, for a period of time, I decided that I would not publish a book at all.

Then, in early 2020, I wrote an essay for an American publication arguing that economic policy actions should be guided by a clearly articulated monetary theory which recognizes the natural order of economic activity. Such a theory would anchor economic measures to the natural world and re-establish the historic connection, only recently forgotten, between money and food.

In that paper, I began to see how my ideas might cohere into a general philosophy of money. This experience inspired me to return to the project. I spent the last two years rewriting and consolidating my original observations into the treatise you are about to read.

Philosophy ought to explain as much as possible in as few words as possible. It has taken many years of reflection to condense these ideas into an accessible book. The brevity with which I present my theory should not be mistaken for a lack of depth or defensibility of its arguments. My objective is to provide the ordinary reader with a simple understanding of the natural laws that govern an economic system, while also providing the seasoned academic with a renewed framework for penetrating beyond the abstruse concepts that cloud economic theory today. I seek to bring us back to the way the first thinkers may have approached the subject while also incorporating thousands of years of acquired knowledge since then.

One of the key insights that guided me in this endeavour was the recognition that certain commonly used economic terms such as "capital", "debt", "interest", "value", and "wealth" have lost their relation to historic economic literature and, by consequence, have lost their meaning. A theory of money that begins from the ground up, from the elementary grammar of nature itself, is required before these lofty terms can descend to their proper context. For this reason, you will not find any mention of these terms within the core body of this work. You will instead find new definitions and principles that I believe to be more fundamental for a true and holistic understanding of money and economics.

With this book, I aim to expound a philosophy of money that will stimulate others, especially young thinkers, public officials, and academics, to build upon the work I have done, so that we might all aspire towards an economic system that produces real prosperity held in the bounds of the natural order.

I advise the reader to treat this book as the definitive explication of my ideas on these topics over and above any prior writings, even when these may appear to contain common threads of thought.

Oxford
July 2022

For thus says the Lord:
"Behold, I will extend prosperity to her like a river, and
the wealth of nations like an overflowing stream;
and you shall suck, you shall be carried upon her hip,
and dandled upon her knees."

Isaiah LXVI, 12

❧ I ❧

Two men rise early in the morning. The first steps out onto his land. The second enters an office building. By noon the first man has tended to his crops; the second man has attended a meeting and has written some code on his computer. Several weeks pass and the first man harvests his maturing crops, selling the product in the local market. The second man repeats the same activity, attending meetings and typing away on his computer. Both men live in the same country, not even many miles away from one another, yet their relationship to the natural world is manifestly different. Men and women who participate in the former type of activity invest their human action directly into nature and, by consequence, produce something tangible that provides sustenance to their community. Men and women of the latter category offer their human action as a service to others. Considering these diverse expressions of activity, it is difficult to see what makes their cooperation in the same economy possible and, more importantly, what makes this cooperation sustainable both naturally and socially. This question may be put in clear terms: Why does the software engineer assume that the farmer will share the food he has produced from nature? Why do we in a modern society expect food from the farmer as if it were a given?

Throughout the course of this treatise, we shall seek to demystify these and other questions relating to human cooperation by progressively discerning the reality of the *natural order*: the system of natural laws that governs individual human action and collective cooperation. We will come to see that, no matter how economically or politically complex our human societies appear, they nevertheless remain accountable to the regularities and vagaries of the natural world. This philosophical investigation will lead us to recognize that the essence, purpose and role of *money* in any cooperative society is to anchor economic systems to the natural order. Finally, we will learn that there is a *natural order of money* itself: there is a prescription which flows from the heart of nature that renders certain moneys superior to others. It is only when our money is a concrete reflection of nature that the collective system can achieve real and sustainable prosperity.

The main distinction between our theory and those of mainstream economics results from a divergence in methodology. The economic theories which are currently employed to guide society are promulgated in the name of science, ostensibly derived from quantitative data and presented to the public as no different from the observations of the chemist or the deductions of the geometer. Economics must have undergone something akin to an alchemical transfiguration if it developed from the "dismal science" of Thomas Carlyle to an immovable aspect of the "universal science" of mathematical certainty and calculable mechanism in less than two hundred years. This is a distinctly modern view, and we must do something at this stage to try our best to eliminate this perspective if we are to approach the subject with a renewed or untainted sense of clarity.

Economics deals precisely with the intersection of nature and human intention, and so it must account for something of the fundamental irreducibility of the natural world and the society which inhabits it. Cooperation between persons cannot be analyzed or abstractly promoted in a mathematical vacuum, removed from the wider ecological environment, and denuded of its tangible and qualitative features. While analysis and synthesis are reverse and even complementary operations in the realm of pure mathematics, if you break the integral economy into its parts, you will never again be able to reconstitute the whole. In other words, speculation and prediction based upon axiomatic formulations and numerical data will never be able to recompose the living, breathing economy which one sought out in the first place. If economics is meant to be the study of the relation of the cooperative society to nature, then one must entirely preoccupy oneself with synthesis.

For this reason, our theory begins with the age-old method of natural philosophy. This method is appropriate for a true economics insofar as it grounds the quest for greater understanding in the direct observation of nature. Much like the biologist, we must begin with the organism itself, and then we may peer inside the body in order to discern how the parts mutually interact in order to contribute to the health and function of the whole. We proceed by observing qualitative facts and sketching out their contours and relations as they are already given in the natural world. These may include facts of a physical, geological, biological or even sociological kind. In this way, we will reflect upon the qualitative data of the natural world and our occupation of it. This method will offer essential insights into what makes an economy possible at all and what, in turn, renders it sustainable.

❧II❧

The *natural order*, *money,* and *time* are intrinsically bound together, such that no part of this triad can truly be comprehended in the absence of the others. We will begin this chapter by meditating upon the third aspect of this tripartite dynamic: *time.*

Time is the condition in which we find ourselves situated. For this reason, it is the very essence of our shared human experience in the world. Temporality is the ontological medium in which we live, act and die; it is the medium in which the natural world grows, bears fruit and decays, in which flowers blossom, mothers age, and the sun sets. As we transition from the fleeting days of our youth to the mature years of adulthood, we learn that time is precious, that it "flies by", and so we ought to spend it wisely. In the words of Walt Whitman, echoing the eternal analogy of Shakespeare's Seven Ages of Man, "the powerful play goes on, and you will contribute a verse."[1] In the context of the natural order, the "powerful play" is the omnipresent force of time, and the "verse" is our individual life, manifest in our inward experience and our external actions.

But what *is* time? Put simply, time is the master to which the whole of existence is subservient. It is the fundamental, superseding law of nature, according to which human life and the natural world together unfold. We exist *in* time, such that we are unable to escape its unceasing, forward pace. Neither are we able to control nor predict the strange and unknown course which the passage of time will follow. Because of its universality and ineffability, the nature of time has persisted as a compelling subject of poetical reflection and philosophical inquiry since antiquity. In the Book of Ecclesiastes, it is written that God has "put a sense of past and future into their minds".[2] Here the author indicates the intimate sense of the passage of time that we all experience by virtue of being human. We know time flown by to reside in the bygone *past*; the time in which we live and act is *present*; and the time that will soon arrive lies beyond in the *future*.[3] The present is that which is immediately available to my sense-perception; I can immediately engage with or act upon it. The future is that which I anticipate or expect in light of the imminent flight of the present. Finally, the past is that which is no longer alive but remains partially available to me through the dynamic of recollection or remembrance. The individual always lacks the power to change the past, the power to know the future, and the power to, in any way, pause or measure the present as time flows onwards.

There are two basic facts or qualities about the nature of time which therefore appear immediately to us: (1) time moves forward; and (2) time is irreversible. No human effort can possibly change the directionality of time's movement, just as no human effort can succeed in arresting time or physically returning to an episode of its flow which has already passed. In light of this basic philosophical exploration, we can formulate a definition of time which will serve us throughout this inquiry.

> *Definition I. **Time**. Time is the ultimate law of nature which saturates all things. It is universal, personal and qualitative, and it is forward-flowing and irreversible.*

This understanding of time is self-evident by way of common sense reasoning about ordinary life. Simply put, one's individual actions are beholden to the requirements of the present: if you are hungry, you must find food to eat; if you are cold, you must find a source of heat; if you are walking across a busy street, you must avoid the cars in the way. While the daydreaming recluse can sit alone and indulge in his fond memories all day, at some point he must recoil to the present in order to answer its given circumstances with the reply of perfunctory action. The moment that the daydreamer needs to eat, he will be pulled away from his subjective idealizations into the hard reality of perception and action, whereupon he must get up, move about, locate some food, and refuel his body.

We begin by recognizing this ontological reality because all cooperation, life and activity take place within time. Contemporary economics tends to ignore the condition of our temporality by transforming economic activity into measurable and quantitative data which appear simultaneous and thus essentially predictable. Our method, by contrast, is the temporal method. When thinking about the economic system in the unavoidable context of time, we look more to temporal dependency, to antecedents and consequents, rather than to abstracted simultaneities. Before looking to what motivates an action within the cooperative system, we have to first look at what allows that action to occur in the first place. In other words, both the natural world and human action are subordinate to this reality of time. This understanding of our temporal condition will lead us to a greater comprehension of both the natural requirements and the generated products of human cooperation. We will now turn to investigate the other essential features of the natural order which emerge within the omnipresent theatre of time.

❧III❧

Nature as a whole is fundamentally a thermodynamic system. When we observe the material effects of ongoing time, we can discern the presence of two distinct natural forces that regulate worldly change. The first of these forces is *energy*, which is the *generative* force present in nature: energy propels the formation and ordering of matter, the life and growth of organisms, and the construction and resilience of human systems. Simply think of energy as the blooming of a rose in springtime. The counterpart of energy is *entropy*, which is the *degenerative* force present in nature: entropy compels matter, life and institutions towards disorder, death, and decay, finally causing complex matter to return to its elemental substances. Simply think of entropy as the withering of that same rose. Like everything else in the world, the forces of energy and entropy are soaked in and directed by the irreversible flow of time.[4]

Our observation of the natural world reveals that energy and entropy are interdependent, meaning that they are perpetually engaged in a cyclical relationship as time unfolds. We deliberately avoid describing energy as "creative" and entropy as "destructive" for the reason that energy can neither be created nor destroyed in the physical world; energy can only be conserved. Matter itself can neither be created nor destroyed, but merely changes as energy and entropy act upon it. In other words, the cycle of generation and degeneration does not entail total creation nor total annihilation. Any system is thermodynamic insofar as it is characterized by this process of energy conservation in the face of entropy through time. We may now formulate the thermodynamic law of energy and entropy as follows.

> *Definition II.* **The thermodynamic law of energy and entropy**. *Energy and entropy are countervailing and interdependent forces that universally act upon all matter in time. Consequently, all change in the natural world is thermodynamic, characterized by the conservation of energy in the face of entropy and expressed in natural cycles of generation and degeneration.*

Before we proceed, it is important to note that this definition and manner of speaking about energy and entropy differ from that of the physicist, chemist, or even the economist. This is because we simply seek to observe and contemplate the overarching dynamic of these prepotent forces without attempting to identify their essential constitution or internal structure. Along these lines, we can reason that energy is the source of life, movement, activity, and heat. Unlike time, which can be grasped intuitively yet can never be measured by physical instruments, the conservation of energy is a measurable activity in the form of movement and in the form of heat.[5] We call this activity *metabolization*. This activity is present in the flame burning wood in a campfire; it is present in the air through the phenomenon of wind, which can be harnessed to power a windmill; it is present in the plant which soaks up sunlight and water in order to grow; and it is present in microscopic bacteria which metabolize caloric energy in order to propel cellular motility.

Metabolization is most visibly observed in animal and human bodies. From the moment that we wake in the morning, we begin to expend the energy that we conserved by eating and sleeping. We must then eat in order to conserve more energy to expend throughout the day, and so on and so forth. The simple fact that we *must* eat and *must* sleep in order to maintain our vitality reveals that the body is a thermodynamic system which is constantly subject to the dynamic interplay between generation and deterioration. In the case of living organisms, biological metabolism is the sum of the processes that convert energy through a chain of physical-chemical reactions in order to provide life and movement to the body; this energy is given in the form of food and water.

We resist, however, speaking of the process of metabolization in strictly biological terms. We rather choose to apply the term metabolization to all thermodynamic processes which conserve and expend energy, because all thermodynamic systems require an energy source for the activity of that system. Both the fire and the organism alike require an energy source in order to sustain their active processes. In the process of burning coal, for example, the energy conserved in the coal is expended into heat which can be harnessed for motion, as in the case of the steam engine. Likewise, a solar panel conserves the energy of the sun through photovoltaic cells which produce an electric current. In all these instances, be they biological or mechanical, we observe the presence of a near-metaphysical and seemingly magical feature of our natural world which we implicitly take for granted: that energy is always and constantly conserved from an external source, expended, and re-conserved.

Non-biological sources of energy are called *fuels*. Biological sources of energy are called *foods*.[6] The thermodynamic system must constantly metabolize these sources of energy if the system is to endure and continue to operate. Without food, the human body lacks the nutritive sustenance it requires to live. Without fuel, the machine ceases to function.

There is, furthermore, a third energy source which permeates the natural world and serves to administer the more vital sources of foods and fuels. We call this energy source *primary materials* or *elemental substances*. When we conceptualize thermodynamic systems in the abstract, we might conceive of foods and fuels as the only concrete energy sources. In reality, however, foods and fuels are harvested as energy sources through the aid of elemental substances. A basic example of this is how the growth of crops is effectuated by the addition of phosphorus in the form of animal manure or crop residue. The farmer additionally uses a hoe or scythe fashioned from iron in order to tend to his land. The necessity of elemental substances as energy sources is more apparent in the case of machines, as the steam engine or the solar panel cannot exist without the elements which are their necessary components. In this way, matter in general, as it is concretized in basic elements, enables the thermodynamic flow of energy through its form or physicality.

The central consequence of this exploration of the thermodynamic law of energy and entropy is that foods, fuels, and elementary materials serve as the concrete embodiments of energy, as the sources of life and movement within the natural order. This understanding, situated within the greater context of irreversible temporality, explains why a person who is starving will die, why a car that is empty of fuel will not drive, why a computer without silicon will not be able to compute, and so on. While this may seem like a banal insight, it is essential to approach the question of human cooperation and economics according to these overarching dynamics which govern the natural order. We must now turn to appreciate human cooperation itself as a thermodynamic system which is temporally and energetically dependent upon foods, fuels, and primary materials.

❧IV❧

The continual conservation and expenditure of energy sources is the underlying dynamic that sustains human life and human cooperation in time. In this way, all human action and coaction is powered by the repeated production and consumption of foods, fuels, and primary materials. For now, let us not dispute that everyone consumes energy in these forms and subsequently does something with that energy. When we eat food, we expend this energy in the form of one activity or another: a mother nurses her baby, a farmer tends to his crops, a philosopher writes a book. This phenomenon of expending the energy that we have conserved from nature into some external output is what we call the *product* of our human action. If our ingested energy must be conserved back into the world after we have released it, then it must be conserved *in* something, namely, the product of our activity. This is the physical expression of the law of energy and entropy at the individual level of the economy, as our personal contribution to the wider environment.

But we must zoom out from the personal level to that

of the cooperative system if we are to understand how we achieve and maintain energy sources in order to fulfil these activities in the first place. Man begins by cooperating with his environment in the present in order to extract food for the future. Once consumed, the food is already in the past, meaning that it has begun its entropic path through digestion and caloric expenditure (or, if not consumed, through rot and decay). The life of the present exacts more energy in order to be sustained, such that man must perpetually work to maintain and regenerate his food supply now and into the future. The incessant pulse of time and the countervailing forces of energy and entropy thus require that humanity must continuously interact with nature in order to survive. It is only when a surplus of food is achieved and continuously maintained that an economic system can persist through time as well as increase in complexity.

We have just begun to sketch out the more complex *chain of temporal energy dependency* that governs an economy. If we take a closer look, the most important agent who emerges in this vast causal scheme is the individual who deals directly with nature in order to produce the food that is our lifeblood. Consider, for example, a farmer, forager, fisherman, or hunter. These primary actors must negotiate, as it were, with the natural order. They must respond to nature's changing circumstances and correct their course of action in the face of her generative and degenerative cycles. When these negotiations are successful, the products of their activity feed the greater society with metabolic energy. Both the temporal and thermodynamic laws enforce the *primacy* of these individuals within any economic system, because it is only through their efforts to produce food (followed by, in a post-subsistence society, their decision to share it with others) that any other activities within the economy can be initiated and sustained. The food that is necessary for all life and movement is the direct result of the farmer's repeated, laborious, and persistent negotiations with nature in the present and into the future.

Farmers, hunters, and their ilk mediate energy sources in the form of foods from the natural world into the greater economy. There are two further kinds of primary cooperators who likewise serve as emissaries of the natural order in correspondence to the two additional categories of energy sources: fuels and primary materials. As we just noted, the chain of temporal and energetic succession in any economy begins with the *food producers*, such as the farmer and hunter, who act as the first cause of survival and surplus. Next in this chain come the *fuel producers* of the economic system, such as the lumberjack or coal miner, who follow the farmers. They work to harvest non-nutritive energy sources from nature which provide heat and motion. The tertiary members within this primary network are the *elemental producers* such as the miner for metals. The product of their activity is a tangible good which is employed as a necessary input in the preceding types of primary activity. In a simple or subsistence economy, it is conceivable that the three roles may be intertwined to such a degree that they can be carried out by one and the same person. As the economy grows in scale and complexity, however, we begin to perceive the implicit distinction between the three roles. In any case, the tripartite kinds of activity exhibited by the primary economy reciprocally influence each other and work together to provide the society with its surplus of energy.

What unifies the three kinds of primary cooperators is their direct connection to the natural world because they produce the fruits of the earth through the work of their human hands. In other words, their activity is a deliberate response to and engagement with the generative and degenerative cycles of the natural order. The products of their activity are the foods, fuels, and primary materials which we require as energy sources. These products arise from nature and can be weighed, divided and shared with others. We call these products *energy embodiments*.[7]

> *Definition III. **Energy embodiments**. The products of human activity produced via direct negotiation with the natural world, embodied in foods, fuels, and basic elements. These products can be weighed, divided and shared with others. Energy embodiments are the fundamental currencies of cooperation.*

Without food, fuel, and basic elemental substances, there would be no source of life and motion to sustain the other members of the economy. We previously described these three components as energy sources that are indispensable to metabolization in thermodynamic systems.

Our definition of energy embodiments, however, allows us to directly relate these energy sources with the human activity required to harvest or produce them. The heart of any economic system consists in this dynamic production and exchange of energy embodiments as the fundamental currencies of cooperation both naturally (from the natural world to humans) and socially (between different members of a society).

All other activities in any cooperative system follow behind the nodes which produce energy embodiments. We call this secondary segment of economic actors the *service economy*. The service economy is composed of individuals who are dependent upon the surplus of energy embodiments produced by the primary or *real economy*, but who do not contribute to the production of these energy embodiments themselves. Those who qualify as members of the real economy are those who produce more energy embodiments than they consume for their own self-sustenance through aforementioned activities such as farming or mining. The members of the service economy consume, refashion, or redistribute the tangible goods generated by the real economy; by consequence, the product of their activity is a service offered to others. Taken together, the real and service economies form the totality of any human cooperative system.

> *Definition IV.* **The two levels of the human cooperative system.** *The* **real economy** *is the segment of the cooperative system that engages in the production of energy embodiments beyond*

> *the producers' individual needs. The **service***
> ***economy** is the segment of the cooperative system*
> *that engages in occupations and industries that*
> *do not produce and, therefore, solely consume*
> *energy embodiments from the real economy.*

While the real and service economies are both consumers of energy embodiments, there is a critical distinction insofar as the latter segment consumes these energy sources and yet never produces them. For this reason, the service economy is always and everywhere dependent on the activity and products of the real economy.

Let us grant the necessity and precedence of the real economy in producing energy embodiments for all members of the cooperative system. When a person consumes food, they conserve energy from nature and subsequently expend this energy through both their internal vital processes and their outward action in the world. Two options present themselves: either the individual can act to produce more energy embodiments by investing their time and labour back into nature, or they can act to produce something which is *not* an energy embodiment. In the case of the former option, the farmer uses his conserved energy to tend to his crops throughout the day. Here the energy which the farmer expends is conserved again in the form of the products of his toil—he has translated former energy embodiments into renewed ones.[8] For the farmer, a perfect cycle of conservation and expenditure ensues: his energy is conserved in nature in the form of new crops that the farmer himself will consume in the future as an energy source, which he will later expend to labour on his future crops, and so on. In the case of the latter option, the individual chooses to utilize the energy embodiments generated by the real economy to provide a service to others. Examples include the industrialist who uses energy embodiments to manufacture goods such as semiconductor chips, cars or computers; the software engineer who uses energy embodiments to build a website; or the professor who uses energy embodiments to express ideas to his students. People who choose this kind of activity are members of the service economy because they consume from an existing surplus of energy which they do not produce.

Consider a simple test which demonstrates the reality of this claim. Ask yourself the following question: Which industries could engage in a systematic strike without significantly damaging the vitality of the cooperative society? A politician can strike for weeks and months, as sometimes happens during government shutdowns. But if the farmer, the fuel energy producer, or the miner strikes for more than a few days, then the resilience and prosperity of the entire society becomes threatened. Without a constant flow of energy embodiments from nature to the wider economy, members of the service economy are forced to revert to more primary forms of cooperation: for example, an accountant becomes a tiller of the soil. Depending on the severity of the decline in the flow of energy embodiments, the whole of humanity may even return to subsistence societies until a surplus is restored. In this way, the interval between the real and service economies reflects the potential oscillations between subsistence and post-subsistence.

We have just outlined three important distinctions between the real and service economies. First, the real economy produces and consumes energy embodiments, while the service economy only consumes them; thus the service economy is temporally and energetically dependent on the real economy. Second, the activity of the real economy is expressed in cyclical conservation and expenditure of energy embodiments, while the activity of the service economy is characterized by one-way expenditure with no possibility for re-conservation or renewal. Third, the continuous activity of the real economy is the necessary precondition for the possibility of manifold service economy occupations, and for the possibility of entering a state of societal resilience and post-subsistence.

But there is a still deeper and more essential distinction from which all these differences have their origin: unlike the service economy, the real economy answers only to nature. In the real economy, man explores nature, comes to learn her limits, and respectfully works within these boundaries for the benefit of himself and others. This real economy, which is the foundation of every peaceful and prosperous society, operates according to the natural mysteries of generation and degeneration: nature cyclically dies and renews itself, providing us with the privilege of prospering with her seasons. This means that the real economic participants must cooperate with nature according to a *standard of measure and reward* which flows from the natural order itself.

*Definition V. **The natural standard of measure and reward**. Members of the real economy are subject to a standard, imposed by nature, which necessitates that they must repeatedly nego-tiate with and labour within nature's cycles of generation and degeneration. Nature then gives an objective measure and reward to real economic activity in the form of a weight of energy embodiments.*

We cannot harvest a crop at the wrong time, lazily neglect a flock of sheep, or mine for rare substances where they do not exist without incurring some kind of loss. On the contrary, the good shepherd or the hard-working farmer will reap the rewards of nature's surplus. Further-more, the rewards and punishments of nature are always given objectively as a measure of weight: a good harvest simply weighs more than a bad harvest. The quality and quantity of the harvest reflects the farmer's willingness to cooperate with nature's predictable cycles and unpre-dictable whims. The natural order supplies this standard and imposes it upon him; it is a standard which he must accept and work within if he is to survive and prosper.

Put simply, the natural standard means that there is a primary and objective judgement of nature upon the actions of the real economy. Notions of good and bad work, of success and failure, are derived from the farmer's inescapable accountability to this natural standard. His adaptation to the ways of nature leads to an implicit understanding of which actions are practical or impractical, introducing a set of ideals and practices that empower collective and intergenerational knowledge of how to best prosper in the natural world. Such ideals include those of *savings*, producing more than we consume; *frugality*, consuming only what we need; and *preservation*, protecting the land and its resources for the benefit of our children.[9]

This kind of relationship to nature is the true meaning of sustainability: it requires every member of society to view our land and its products as sacred, that is to say, that they exist prior and posterior to the whimsical thoughts and ideas of man. It also requires that we view ideation, which is the trade of the service economy, as always and everywhere accountable to the real economy.

We began this chapter by establishing that the human cooperative system itself is thermodynamic. All economies, no matter their size, are powered by the animating force of energy embodiments. A surplus of energy is achieved and maintained through the dynamic production and exchange of energy embodiments, introducing a chain of temporal energy dependency in which the real economy serves the principal and primary role. We shall now discover how accountability to the natural order and to its given standard of measure and reward is the architectonic principle of all human cooperative systems.

V

As the mediator between man and the generative force of nature, the real economy is dependent directly and ultimately upon the natural order, upon its gifts and punishments, upon its blessings and maledictions, as it toils to produce energy embodiments for the whole economy. The real economy must therefore learn to work with nature, and its success or failure is measured by nature's physical rewards. The service economy is temporally and energetically dependent on this activity because it does not produce energy embodiments.[10] Consequently, even though members of the service economy are not directly measured and rewarded by the natural standard itself, they are nonetheless accountable to it. We call this fundamental connection between humans and the natural world *ecological accountability*:

> *Definition VI.* **Ecological accountability**. *All members of a cooperative system are accountable to the natural standard of measure and reward. The real economy is directly subject to*

*this standard. The service economy is subject to
it indirectly because its members are temporally
and energetically dependent on the activity of
the real economy.*

Ecological accountability expresses the fact that the cooperative system is always and everywhere tethered to the natural order and to our necessity of negotiating with it in order to produce the energy embodiments that we need. When we eat breakfast, when we start up our cars to drive to work, when we open our laptops and begin to type, we are implicitly involving ourselves in the natural order and its standard of measure and reward. We are taking in the maintenance of the land, the tilling of the soil, the sowing of the seeds, the days of rain and sun, and the long hours of harvest. The farmer is told by nature how and when his crops can be grown. We participate in this edict each time we partake of this harvest for our own purposes of activity. No service economy is self-sufficient, just as no man is an island. We cannot live without nature's reward, just as our bodies cannot survive without breathing in the oxygen that surrounds us.

No matter how complex our human societies appear, they therefore always remain ecologically accountable to the standard that nature imposes upon its mediators in the real economy. The moment that somebody in the service economy consumes energy embodiments for a certain activity, whether it be creating, engineering, or manufacturing, his or her activity is immediately dependent upon the generation of energy embodiments from nature by the real economy, and upon the willing exchange of these energy embodiments from the primary cooperator to the greater economy. Ecological accountability is thus a fact of nature which governs all individual and collective action. It is the underlying and guiding principle of all cooperation and sustainable prosperity.

The total scheme of ecological accountability may be illustrated as a circle. At the centre of the circle is the point of contact between the real economy and the natural order. Dotted along the periphery of the circle are the points which represent the service economy. As the radius connects these peripheral points to their circular centre, so is the service economy inextricably anchored to the real economy and to the natural order. The relationship between the real and service economies, understood in this way, is intrinsically symbiotic because of the concrete, radial bind between them. It is therefore not a relationship of implicit hostility or mutual contention. Both segments of society may very well work together by drawing upon the collective surplus to empower outward manifestations of the will, making industries, occupations, and forms of leisure possible that would be effectively impossible if all members of the economy were engaged directly in the real economy—just as a circle would not be a circle if there were only a central point.

As generative cycles of energy embodiments radiate from the centre to the periphery of the greater economy, and as the economic system grows in complexity and scale, the possibility arises for those peripheral points to turn away, as it were, from their centre and neglect the radii which connect them to their core. In this case, ecological accountability remains the guiding principle of cooperation as a matter of fact even while it is over-looked or ignored. This forgetting of accountability is only possible because the service economy possesses the ability to temporarily decouple itself from the natural order for the very reason that it lies at the periphery of its generative and degenerative cycles. The real economy, on the other hand, enjoys no such luxury, for it is dependent upon nature's commandments. What follows from ignoring this reality is an unnatural view of prosperity as something which can be mastered, determined, and distributed according to the personal desires and subjective ideals of the service economy. It is then that the relationship between the real and service economies becomes *parasitic*.

In a parasitic system, the service economy demands energy embodiments from the real economy irrespective of nature's limits and cycles, thereby attempting to circumvent or transcend the natural standard which governs the success and failure of the real economy. The result of this attempted divorce from ecological account-ability threatens the sustainable relationship between humanity and nature, and the symbiotic relationship between the real and service economies. On the one hand, the activity of the real economy remains bound to the requirements of nature: a bad harvest may cause the farmer to fail to produce a crop, or geological scarcity of ore may prevent a miner from carrying out further operations. On the other hand, members of the service economy can use their education, their ideas, and their power to dominate the real economy.[11] In such inverted economic systems, ecological accountability nevertheless persists *de facto*, and degeneration (or consumption) rather than generation (or conservation) becomes the guiding principle of cooperation. The parasitic economy promotes a delusive sense of prosperity in which inequity is felt by many, but which is disguised as "progress" by abstract measures such as "aggregate demand", "gross domestic product" and "nominal growth". In other words, while ecological accountability is always the architectonic principle of cooperation, it can nevertheless be manipulated or hidden from view by the service economy.

The divorce of economic activity from ecological accountability can only ever be temporary. Generative cycles within the natural order can unfold over many years or even decades. Parasitic states of cooperation may therefore persist for periods as long as a human lifespan. These parasitic systems, over the long run, will always prove to be *unsustainable* precisely because they have forgotten the ecological accountability to which all are beholden. The natural order will eventually exert its force and be felt again by the periphery, often at great cost to the whole of society and its culture. The events leading to the Fall of the Roman Empire, the French Revolution, and the Great Depression come to mind as familiar historical examples.

Every member of the economic system is primarily and ultimately ecologically accountable to the natural order. In a complex and growing cooperative system, economic activity must always and everywhere be bound to this prepotent principle, if people are to prosper sustainably in relation to one another and in relation to the natural world. This requires something concrete, communicated at every point of the economy, to align human agency and ambition with the natural order to which it belongs, thereby ensuring that notions of prosperity can never be divorced from the natural standard which governs the real economy. In other words, the natural standard itself must be reified and extended to all members of the cooperative system. This extension of the standard would ensure that ecological accountability remains at the heart of cooperation, protecting against its being forgotten or ignored, and it would thus guarantee that the activity of the periphery always remains bound to the real economy which sits at the central point of contact with the natural order.

❧VI❧

Our investigation has helped us so far to elucidate certain key principles of human cooperation. We first learned that man and the world he inhabits exist in time. We then learned that man cooperates with the generative and degenerative cycles of nature, which can neither be vanquished nor eluded. By consequence, energy embodiments are produced, shared, and consumed as the fundamental currencies of cooperation in any economic system. The real economy is that segment which mediates energy embodiments to the greater economy by working within the natural standard of measure and reward. As the economy grows in scale and complexity, there emerges a reciprocal desire between every individual member of society to exchange the various products they have or services they can render for the energy embodiments they need. All that we have learned has led us to appreciate that all members of an economy are accountable to each other in relation to the natural world. If its members desire to cooperate sustainably, then they must place ecological accountability at the heart of their economic system.

Perhaps, on a human level, we may think of ecological accountability as a faithful respect for nature's limits and edicts, and for those who work directly within these parameters. To be accountable in this sense would thus require the natural limits themselves to be discerned. But these limits are not posited *by us*, they are prescribed *by it*—by the natural order—and are only discovered by or revealed to us. Ecological accountability is not, therefore, simply a shared ideal or notional promise. It is rather something which is confirmed, concretized, and exchanged among all actors and at all points of the economic system. Understood in these terms, it seems that we are touching upon the nature, purpose, and role of *money* itself in the economy, as a common *measure* and *reward* which reflects the standard imposed upon the real economy by the natural order itself.

The essence of money is like a mirror: it reflects ecological accountability at all points within the economic system. Money serves to extend the natural standard from the fixed point of contact between man and nature at the level of the real economy to all members of the diverse economic system. In this way, money anchors notions and ideals of prosperity to the objective accountability of the real economy, to the natural pulse of energy embodiments, by ensuring that the whole society measures and rewards activity relative to these dynamic cycles of generation and degeneration. A money which reflects ecological accountability ensures that when the real economy does well by cooperating with nature, the greater economy also prospers; and when the real economy does poorly, so, too, does the greater economy suffer.

If we are to pierce through this philosophical outline of the nature of money, we will see that we ultimately seek to describe something which is simultaneously a measure and reward. We seek a *measure* of human action relative to the natural order, and a *reward* for action in the same way that nature deems the acts of the real economy to be successful or not. In the preceding chapters, we learned that the fundamental currencies of cooperation are energy embodiments: the food we eat, the fuel which propels us forward, and the elements and materials which allow all life and work to be possible. In these energy embodiments, we uncover something tangible that arises from the natural world and already serves *in itself* as both a measure and reward for the activity of the primary cooperator who toiled for it. If we consider the farmer again, a present harvest is judged good or bad because its weight is *measured* relative to a past season's harvest, or to a different farmer's harvest in the same season. At the same time, the harvest itself, good or bad, is an objective *reward* given by nature. Thus, the essential nature of energy embodiments, having this dual property which itself reflects the natural standard of measure and reward, allows any one embodiment to serve as a common measure and reward for another.

If money is to serve as a common measure and reward of cooperation which itself reflects and extends the natural standard, then it must be as real as the food we eat, as real as the fuel which propels us forward, as real as the substances which we uncover in the earth—as real, in a word, as nature itself. It is precisely because the real economy produces the energy embodiments upon which the whole economy depends that the measure and reward must be *of the same kind* as the standard which determines the success or failure of the real economy. In other words, in order for the software engineer to cooperate according to the same standard imposed on the farmer, his money must be something *like* the good or bad harvest. Money must therefore be an energy embodiment. We are now ready to introduce our definition of money:

> *Definition VII.* **Money.** *Money is an energy embodiment which serves as a common measure and a reward for economic activity. Money extends the natural standard imposed upon the real economy to all members of an economic system, promoting cooperation while reflecting ecological accountability as its guiding principle.*

This definition of money may, at first, appear quite unusual compared to the explanations that we are given in economic theory today. It is important for us to briefly engage with these ideas in order to understand how our conclusion about the nature of the economy and the role of money within it, following directly from our study of the natural order, essentially differs from these standard accounts.

In 1875, William Stanley Jevons published an essay on the monetary systems of the world entitled *Money and the Mechanism of Exchange*.[12] Since then, it has become *de rigueur* for any discussion about money to revolve around the terms that Jevons (borrowing from Aristotle and Locke) employed in his treatise. These include defining money as a "unit of account", "medium of exchange" and "store of value" (and, to a lesser extent, "standard of value"). We agree with Jevons when he states that exchange is "the barter of the comparatively superfluous for the comparatively necessary" and therefore, because of its functions, money promotes efficient cooperation.[13] By selling their products and services for money, the farmer and the software engineer can each acquire the things they need from those who have it. Our definition of money captures these functions by saying that money is a common measure and reward.

Our understanding departs from Jevons and the thinkers who follow in his tradition insofar as we recognize that ecological accountability places a concrete limit upon human desires. In this way, the exchange of the comparatively superfluous for the comparatively necessary reflects something more than just a "a ratio between two numbers".[14] Furthermore, we have shown that the usefulness of energy embodiments is something intrinsic that arises from their physical qualities.[15] By defining money as an energy embodiment, we identify the essence of money beyond its function of promoting efficient cooperation by identifying it as that which inherently reflects ecological accountability. In this sense, we also depart from the traditional understanding of the terms "store" or "standard of value". By anchoring economic activity to the natural standard of measure and reward, we place less emphasis on the personal desire to own something for its own sake over long periods of time, and instead place a greater emphasis on the collective desire to cooperate sustainably. In our definition, money is a long-term store of value to the farmer and the software engineer because it is a common measure and reward that arises from the natural standard.

In light of this difference, we argue that the terms historically used to define money become enigmatic when divorced from an understanding of the natural order. At best, they are incidental descriptions of the functions of money, which can be easily refashioned or reinterpreted to mean different things. In our times, these exact words are used to describe anything from digital data, to works of art, to investment securities. While these things may promote efficient cooperation or be desired as storehouses of value, they do not reflect ecological accountability. By contrast, our natural philosophy has allowed us to observe that the true nature of money is more than the sum of its functions.

Many thinkers have also proposed that money is a social contract, a legal fiction that binds human beings together and according to which some freedoms are ceded to the state in return for justice and security. Money in this system is a man-made standard agreed to in order to promote even-handed cooperation, specialization, and intra-personal accountability. This aspect of money as a kind of societal glue is also true, but it only helps us to understand certain sociological or anthropological features arising from the adoption of a monetary system. We have learned that the more important "glue" function of money is that it binds the wider economy to the actions of the real economy, so that all economic activity is measured and rewarded in accordance with the fruits of the natural order.

In most contemporary debates, money is understood to be entirely subjective or relative. Both modern economists and anthropologists believe that money is an artefact of the state and is not something useful in and of itself; in other words, money is only useful insofar as the state enforces its use.[16] But they fail to recognize that, in any society that has moved beyond subsistence, energy embodiments are already moving within and throughout the cooperative system as measure and reward.[17] In other words, the impetus for the initial movement from the producer to the consumer is more fundamental than any business relation, state-enforced use, or subjectively determined value, for it reflects the vital impulse to metabolize energy in the face of entropy.[18] It also signifies something beautiful about the role of the real economy in mediating the gift of energy from nature and the members of that economy agreeing to share it with their community.

If money itself is an energy embodiment, it is therefore useful in and of itself. For without energy embodiments there would be no life, movement, or cooperation. As defined earlier, the category of energy embodiments includes foods, fuels, and basic elements. Anthropologists often refer to diverse historical examples of these energy embodiments serving as money across cultures and epochs: almonds, bronze, cacao nuts, corn, cotton, copper, furs, indigo, iron, lead, olive oil, oxen, salt, sheep, tin, tobacco, wheat, and wood have all circulated as money within various societies.[19] While any one of these can be used as money, the question arises as to whether one type of embodiment better serves as the tangible extension of the natural standard, the common measure and reward, and, thus, the mirror of ecological accountability in a post-subsistence society. The question we are now taking up is whether there is a hierarchy of potential moneys or, in other words, whether there is a *natural order of money.*

❧VII❧

Now we must pierce deeper into the heart of the natural order, into all of its irreducible complexity and lawlike regularity, in order to discover which energy embodiment can best serve as money. First, we may reason that the best potential money will be an energy embodiment which is superior in its resistance to entropy through time. In other words, it will maintain its material weight through time in the most energy efficient manner; it will endure as it was produced without requiring an additional expenditure of energy for its preservation. This money would truly be a part and product of nature, and yet it would outlast the effects of deterioration better than most natural things, thus rendering it a reliable extension of the natural standard which can measure and reward all acts of cooperation at all moments of time. The pithy adage "time is money" is indeed true insofar as money, like time, must persist from the past, through the present and into the future.

Second, we may reason that, within the constellation of available energy embodiments, the superior choice to serve as money would be that which is difficult to obtain from nature. By difficulty, we mean that more energy embodiments are required to produce a weight of it than others. This money would reflect the upper limit of the natural standard of measure and reward and correspondingly serve as the fixed measure or apex against which all lower limits of difficulty are relatively ordered and measured. As we shall soon learn, both qualities are a function of *natural scarcity*, an objective feature of the natural order.

The two qualities which we have just outlined, (1) *resistance to entropy* and (2) *difficulty or rarity*, serve as the price of admission for an energy embodiment to be considered as the upper limit within the natural order of money. Foods and fuels, though essential energy embodiments, are subject to the immediate effects of entropy in either their imminent consumption or eventual decay. Accordingly, in a society that has moved beyond subsistence, a superior money will be neither food nor fuel.

The remaining energy embodiments to consider are either pure elements or compounds of pure elements. While compounds can be broken down into their constituents, the pure elements themselves cannot be further reduced through ordinary chemical reactions, meaning that they are simple, basic and homogeneous units of matter.[20] These fungible or mutually interchangeable elements are rightly described as the fundamental "building blocks" of all matter, as the raw material of corporeal reality. The pure elements are the only truly unitary substances which cannot be created by human effort, and which must therefore be extracted from nature through the expenditure of energy embodiments. If money is to be an energy embodiment which is harvested from nature itself (like foods and fuels) but which is resistant to entropy (unlike foods and fuels), then the only remaining option is for money to be elemental.

To uncover the upper limit and the relative ranking of potential moneys within the natural order, we need not look much farther than the periodic table. Of the 118 elements which the scientific community has come to recognize at the date of writing this book, 94 can be said to occur naturally on earth.[21] Included in this list are six elements that occur in extreme trace quantities. This leaves us with 88 elements found in nature in non-extreme trace quantities.[22]

Pure elements exhibit unique physical attributes which are intrinsic to their individual nature, causing any one element to differ in its qualities and potentialities from another. These attributes or properties include natural forms, qualitative appearance such as colour and texture, specific weights or gravities, relative electronegativity, conductivity, reactivity with air, antimicrobial effects, and crustal abundance. These unchanging properties render the individual nature of each element uniquely observable, measurable, and predictable. The fact that each element exhibits idiosyncratic qualities is a phenomenon of the natural order that we call *natural scarcity*:

> *Definition VIII.* **Natural scarcity.** *Pure elements exhibit unchanging properties which delimit their reality and their potentiality.*

Natural scarcity dictates that we cannot find anything else in nature other than what is already given, how it is given, and in the amount that it is given.[23] So, for example, if we want to find something in nature with which we can fashion a tool, we have to find a ductile solid of a certain weight with an accessible melting point.

We will now investigate the intrinsic features of the elements in relation to whether they fulfil the above qualities which we seek for our money: *resistance to entropy* and *difficulty*. The first of the characteristics which dictates whether an element is resistant to entropy is the category of natural forms. The elements exhibit three forms: solid, liquid, and gaseous. We may look to solids alone for the simple and practical reason that our money must be tangible. Solids come in two forms: either they are brittle or ductile. Brittle solids break into bits when met with force, making it difficult if not impossible for them to endure without change. Ductile solids will deform when met with tensile force while retaining their volumetric weight. Gold and lead are the most ductile of the solids, while bismuth and beryllium are the most brittle. Malleability is similar to ductility in that it reflects an element's capacity to retain its volumetric weight when met with compressive force. It is important to note that not all ductile solids are malleable: gold, silver, aluminium, copper, tin, lead, and zinc are the most malleable of the ductile solids. Elements which are naturally stable and solid yet brittle cannot function as money because they would be unable to maintain their material existence in the form of their weight. Rhodium, for example, becomes extremely brittle when one tries to handle or work with it, thus rendering it impractical as a shared money. In sum, our money must be a solid which is ductile or malleable.

Reactivity with air is also an essential quality when considering resistance to entropy. This denotes whether an element is stable, toxic, or volatile at room temperature, as well as whether the element reacts with oxygen or other gases. Most naturally occurring elements react with air, meaning that they form oxide compounds and are thereby subject to entropy through oxidation, rust, explosion, and so on. A familiar example is iron: when exposed to air, iron becomes the chemical compound iron oxide, meaning that it transforms over time from its pure elemental form into rust. Similarly, the surface of shiny copper roofs transforms into verdigris. The tendency to react with air renders iron, copper, and other metals inferior as potential moneys. There are only four naturally occurring elements which remain stable when exposed to air. These are known as the *precious metals*: gold, silver, platinum, and palladium.[24]

Turning now to the second criterion of difficulty, we can look to the significant attribute of an element's physical rarity, known today by the scientific term "crustal abundance". Our observation of this phenomenon is the product of thousands of years of exploring for and extracting elements from the ground, as attested to by the millions of holes drilled into the earth throughout the ages. Through the lens of crustal abundance, we learn that there exists a pre-given relationship between the elements in terms of their relative presence in the earth's surface. Oxygen (which is used by plant roots and soil microbes for respiration) is the most abundant element therein; likewise, there is more lead found in the earth's surface than gold; there is more sodium and calcium in the ground than copper and nickel; and so on. Our observations of and negotiations with nature reveal that each element physically exists in the earth on this scale of relative abundance when compared with other elements. This is an important metric insofar as it reveals just how *likely* we are to discover and extract certain elements over others, and thus how much energy is required to extract these elements from nature. Looked at from the perspective of man, crustal abundance is nothing more than the difficulty, the amount of time, and the amount of energy embodiments required to discover and extract an element from nature. Looked at from the perspective of the natural order itself, crustal abundance reflects the relative distribution and overall weight of a specific element deposited in the earth. In a word, crustal abundance dictates how *rare* an element is, as a fact of nature itself.

The other properties of the solid elements (electronegativity, melting point, specific gravity, conductivity, etc.) do not necessarily indicate an element's resistance to entropy or its relative rarity or difficulty, but they do express other important and individual aspects of the element such as its usefulness, and so reveal the intricate administration of natural scarcity. The first of these additional qualities is specific gravity or weight. Specific gravity may be understood as the relative density or weight of one element in comparison to another. If you were to place two masses of pure gold and pure silver, both the exact size of a sugar cube, in each hand or on a balance scale, then you would instantly perceive that the identically sized cubes have different weights: the gold is simply heavier than the silver. The metric of specific gravity denotes this basic and immutable property of the intrinsic weight of each element. When factoring in crustal abundance, we can appreciate how a rare element with a higher specific gravity would serve as a superior extension of the natural standard of measure and reward by providing the added benefit of occupying less volume, making it easier to move and share among economic actors.

The melting point of an element refers to the temperature at which it will transform from its naturally occurring state. At 1085 degrees Celsius, for example, copper transforms from its solid state to molten, which is a useful practice for alloying and for creating objects such as statues, pipes and electric coils. An element's electrical or thermal conductivity indicates the likelihood that it will either conduct or disrupt an electric current or heat. Silver, copper and gold are the most electrically conductive metals. Silver is the metal of choice in the production of solar panels. It is also used in the production of printed circuit board contacts, soldering alloys, and batteries. Copper cookware such as tea kettles and Dutch ovens have been used throughout history precisely because copper is a highly conductive metal, meaning that it both heats quickly and retains heat over a longer period when compared with other metals. Because, however, silver forms a tarnish and copper is prone to oxidation, their rate of conductivity is undermined over time. It is for this reason that gold is the preferred conductor in switch and relay contacts, soldered joints, connecting wires, connecting strips, cell phones, and computers. Gold is in fact handled by the average person in the developed world for nearly four hours per day through their use of smartphones and computers.[25]

Elements can also be naturally antimicrobial, meaning that they kill or inhibit the growth of microorganisms such as bacteria, fungi, algae, moulds, and even viruses. Copper, silver, mercury, zinc, and gold are the most antimicrobial of the elements. Copper is used extensively in agriculture and medicine to control and kill microorganisms. Silver is used as an antiseptic for extensive burns as well as to prevent surgical infections. Silver's antibacterial properties are the reason why it has been the preferred material for chalices, cutlery, plates, and tankards for thousands of years. Gold is used in dental inlays and to treat rheumatoid arthritis.

Of the 88 naturally occurring elements, only four of them pass the highest threshold of resistance to entropy and relative rarity for serving as elemental money: the precious metals. Consider this table which provides an overview of these elements and their natural attributes:

FIG 1. PRECIOUS METALS[26]

ELEMENT	NATURAL STATE	CRUSTAL ABUNDANCE (PPM)	SPECIFIC GRAVITY	MELTING POINT (°C)	HARDNESS
Gold	Ductile Solid	0.004	19.32	1065	2.5
Platinum	Ductile Solid	0.005	21.45	1773	3.5
Palladium	Ductile Solid	0.015	12.00	1555	4.75
Silver	Ductile Solid	0.075	10.49	961	2.5

From this initial table of precious elements, it is a relatively easy path towards identifying gold as the apex element within the natural order of money. We can begin with crustal abundance. Gold is clearly rarer than silver as well as palladium, although we do not dispute that, in terms of crustal abundance, gold and platinum are on equal footing. To appreciate why gold is superior to platinum as elemental money, we need to consider which of these precious metals can best maintain its material weight through time without requiring an additional expenditure of energy embodiments. Because of its intrinsic hardness and high melting point, platinum demands a significantly higher expenditure of energy relative to gold each time it is used within an economy. Employing platinum as money would therefore be less energy efficient.

In this chapter, we have learned that there is indeed a natural order of money, meaning that there is a prescription which flows from the natural order itself and renders certain moneys superior to others. Ranking highest within this order is gold, followed closely by the other precious metals such as platinum and silver. Each of these metals may serve to extend the natural standard and reflect ecological accountability within an economy, but gold appears to occupy a special position by virtue of its relative natural scarcity and resistance to entropy.

Precisely because of its unique natural properties, gold has persisted as one of the most treasured and desirable substances on earth since the dawn of human civilization. This is firstly and foremostly because it is the rarest and the longest-lasting energy embodiment. The density of its weight and corresponding ease of transport, its utility for conductivity and the creation of artefacts, its anti-microbial properties, its splendour, radiance, and lustre, are all further benefits and indications of its status as the natural energy embodiment to be exchanged throughout a cooperative society as the prevailing mode of measure and reward.

❧VIII❧

Our philosophical exploration has shown that there is a natural order of money and that gold is the exemplar given by the order of nature. When money is gold, economic activity is anchored to the natural standard of measure and reward imposed upon the real economy, ensuring that human agency and ambition reflects ecological account-ability, and, thus, that cooperation between society and nature is sustainable. The fact that the earliest civiliza-tions historically demonstrated this knowledge over four thousand years ago is a testament that there indeed exists a natural order of money.[27]

Gold is the longest-lasting, the most energy efficient, and the rarest of the possible energy embodiments which nature bequeaths to us. For this reason, it rests at the apex, at the highest summit of difficulty within the natural standard, and so it is able to measure and reward the energy embod-iments which are arrayed beneath it, without competing with them. Gold is a pure element that nature dispenses by weight in exchange for the more abundant, ephemeral, and even more necessary energy embodiments that we require for vitality and movement. The farmer and the gold miner thus share much in common, insofar as they must answer to the natural standard and to the brute facts of nature. While the gold miner is energetically dependent upon the farmer, in a society that has moved beyond subsistence, the gold which the miner harvests serves as the best measure and reward for the food which the farmer harvests. While they both eat the food generated by the farmer, the gold remains and endures as the lasting energy embodiment of the miner, capable of serving as money for and throughout the entire economy.

As gold continues to circulate throughout the economy, measuring and rewarding a complex network of unique, individual activities, it never ceases to reflect the intrinsic limitations of the natural order. It reminds the greater economic system of the primary negotiation between man and nature which must take place if the cooperative society is to exist and to prosper. It renders every participant in the system ecologically accountable by binding their activity to the natural cycles of generation and degeneration mediated by the real economy. Thus, in a generative cycle, a growing surplus of energy embodiments will exist relative to the gold money, signalling the state of abundance from nature and the carrying capacity to support an expansion of service economic activities. Conversely, in a degenerative cycle, a diminishing surplus of energy embodiments will exist relative to the gold money, signalling a state of deficiency from nature and the need to realign economic activity towards the real economy.

As we learned in the previous chapter, natural scarcity will always ensure that, in both generative and degenerative economic cycles, gold will be released in smaller quantities from nature relative to the more fundamental yet ephemeral energy embodiments. For this reason, when money is gold, ecological accountability is concretized at all times and at all places as the guiding principle of cooperation, dynamically adjusting to and reflecting the relationship between the real economy, the service economy, and the natural world. This is nature's way of reminding us that we must always work together, both between people and between people and nature, and that any attempts to master or influence the course of nature will always fail. If we concretely recognize that there is a natural order of money by employing gold as money, then nature will allow us to prosper sustainably with her seasons if we so choose.

Our philosophy of money may be difficult to grasp. It may appear too simple or even too conceptual to the modern reader. This is because we live in an age where the contrived moneys of the service economy are deployed, often injuriously, as the measure and reward for acts of cooperation. By consequence, modern economic theory, relying on these contrivances to make observations and predictions, promotes unsustainable forms of cooperation. Our economists fail to appreciate the dependence of human societies on the natural world, and on the farmers, miners, and energy producers, seeing nature as a machine to be tinkered with in order to obtain efficiencies and nominal growth. Thus, abstract employment, irrespective of whether the vocation is sustainable within the natural order, is seen to be a reliable metric of prosperity. Consequently, every member of the economy is assumed to be a fluid worker who will accept the wages offered to them without protest or recourse to real economic subsistence. Thus, imports of the most fundamental subsistence food and energy products, even from distant lands, are measured equally with local production. And similarly, exports of these same fundamental goods at the highest price are lauded as signs of economic success, without any consideration towards the conservation of these energy sources.

We are only familiar with an ecologically accountable economy either through historical study or through stories of bygone times where young couples could buy a house with their wages, where middle class households were not required to spend the majority of their incomes on housing and food expenses, where even the factory worker could buy a dress or suit from a local seamstress made from higher quality materials than anything offered on the high street now, and so on. With each passing day, the prices of basic things escape the purchasing power of the farmer and the wage earner, while the contrived moneys become concentrated in the hands of the few, who shrewdly and swiftly concretize their nominal wealth into physical assets. These false moneys fail to meet the most basic requirements which the natural order of money exacts from us: that money itself be an energy embodiment. If our money fails to constantly remind us of the natural order and what it requires of us, then we simply forget about ecological accountability and our collective dependence upon the farmer and upon nature.

Within the false monetary paradigm, to be a member of the real economy is looked down upon and even discouraged, precisely because this occupation guarantees no just reward; while the peripheral actors thrive, the farmer is compensated as if he were an afterthought. So farmers and shepherds are persuaded into leaving their familial land to attend university and work in the City; the new generation would rather work menial office jobs than get their hands dirty in nature; and the land which once was tilled and worked for the greater benefit of society is converted into champaign housing for the ultra-rich.[28] Then we appear surprised when a food, fuel, or commodities shortage ensues, and so we attempt to protect ourselves by looking to other countries to feed our own. In this system, we have been conditioned to accept the dyspeptic symptoms of an inverted, degenerative and parasitic economy—symptoms such as inflation, reckless spending, and limitless growth, which have no mirrored counterpart in the natural order itself. We have willingly allowed ourselves to be guided by the subjective desires of the peripheral actors, rather than the objective scarcity of the highest measure given by the order of nature and its rewards and punishments.

We do not understand scarcity anymore and think that we live in an age "beyond scarcity" simply because we have lost our tangible connection to the natural order in the form of elemental money. But even the most radical promises for a future of endless prosperity, utilitarian well-being, and technological dominance cannot replace the role of energy embodiments or the natural scarcity which governs their production in our economy. These neoteric promises will always fall into the trap of alchemy, now so often derided as a naïve and hubristic pursuit of our unsophisticated past.[29]

Environmentalists similarly recognize that the waste and consumption around which our present system revolves is antagonistic to the ways of nature and the humble place which we must occupy within it. But it is impossible for a solution to these ailments to be given by the periphery; the solution itself must radiate from the fixed, central point outwards; it must be given by nature itself and deployed throughout the economy as a whole.

Money is the mirror of ecological accountability in any society. In this way, our money reflects the health and ideals of our human economy. The more reflective and clear the mirror, the more we, as the members of a shared society and culture, can perceive the genuine reflection of our relationship to one another and to the natural world. But if the mirror is tarnished or fogged, the reflection will be distorted, and we will fail to see ourselves situated in relation to the natural world at all. We may then fall into the false belief that we alone are the masters and legislators of the universe. The natural order of money prescribes gold as the perfect mirror which reflects and irradiates the light of ecological accountability from the fixed point of contact between the real economy and nature to all members of the economic system. Because this light is resistant to entropy and to manipulation, it forces those who seek to cooperate meritoriously to step into its luminosity and assess their individual activities in relation to their fellow citizens and in relation to the natural order itself.[30] Those who accept this contract contribute towards real, lasting prosperity; and those who do not, in time, disappear into obscurity.

Three men rise early in the morning. The first steps onto his land. The second descends into a mine. The third enters an office building. By noon, the first man has tended to his crops; the second has produced one gram of gold; and the third has attended a meeting and has written some code on his computer. Several weeks pass, and the surplus of food produced by the first man is sold in the local market for the surplus of gold produced by the second. The third man must likewise be measured and rewarded for his service according to the natural standard, using money that is gold. Or he must change his ways and become a farmer or miner. These men cooperate in a sustainable way both naturally and socially. We can now see that the food we expect in modern society is not merely a given. The software engineer can assume that he will receive food from the farmer only if he is constantly reminded of the natural order by their shared money.

APPENDIX I

In Chapter VII, we examined the phenomenon of natural scarcity as it relates to pure elements, where this feature of the natural order finds its most objective and potent expression. We shall now investigate how natural scarcity applies to energy embodiments such as foods and fuels.

When elements form compounds, be it a food such as lettuce or a fuel such as coal, we observe natural scarcity in a slightly different way from the pure elements. The natural scarcity of foods can be understood through an analysis of (1) time required from sowing to harvest, (2) crop yields, (3) average storage life once harvested, and (4) energy density. The time required from sowing to harvest measures the number of days that must elapse before seeds mature into harvestable crops. Crop yields measure the average weight of specific crop harvests over a period of time relative to the magnitude of land employed. Crop yields may remind us of elemental crustal abundance; however, an important distinction between the two is that crops can be regenerated on the same plot of land while elements are mined from a finite supply of ore. The average storage life of foods stipulates the average time before a given food will rot and lose its metabolic energy density. This metric for foods parallels reactivity to air for the pure elements, insofar as the former alerts us to a given food's rate of change or diminishment, while the latter alerts us to whether or not a given element will form an oxide (or other gaseous) compound which would then be subject to change and diminishment. Finally, the energy density of a given food reveals the caloric embodiment of a food within a given weight. This intrinsic energy density which is unique to each food delimits the potentiality for a food to serve as a biological source of energy.

FIG. 2: NATURAL SCARCITY OF FOODS SHOWN IN TIME REQUIRED FROM SOWING TO HARVEST, CROP YIELDS, STORAGE LIFE AND ENERGY DENSITY[31]

CROP	TIME (DAYS) REQUIRED FROM SOWING TO HARVEST	AVERAGE CROP YIELD (TONNE/ HECT-ARE)[32]	AVERAGE STORAGE LIFE (DAYS) AT 0°C[33]	ENERGY DENSITY IN CALORIES PER OUNCE
Lettuce	45	21	21	4
Tomato	65	38	14	4
Onion	85	50	28	11
Potato	90	21	130	25
Wheat	125	3.42	180	103
Rice	130	3.71	3,000	37

In this collection of data, we perceive the inherent natural scarcity of certain foods. Lettuce, which takes an average of 45 days to grow, yields 21 tons per hectare. It has a storage life of 21 days and an energy density of 4 calories per ounce. Rice, which requires 130 days to grow, yields 3.71 tons per hectare. It has a storage life of 3,000 days and an energy density of 37 calories per ounce.

While this table is not meant to be exhaustive, it is instructive for recognizing that every kind of food is subject to natural scarcity. It helps us to understand why human cooperative systems have always viewed energy-dense foods with a long storage life such as wheat, rice, and potatoes as essential sources of energy. These foods serve as a dietary staple in nearly every culture because they provide a greater amount of energy for each individual and for the collective when compared with other foods which could potentially be grown in their place.

Our exploration of the natural scarcity of foods provides further support to our discussions about the natural standard of measure and reward and ecological accountability. No matter how much food is desired by the service economy, there are inescapable realities which govern the actions of the real economy. For the farmer to produce food embodying a certain energy density, a specific amount of land is required, a period of time must elapse from sowing to harvest and the harvested weight will have a given storage life before it rots. These are limits imposed upon the farmer by the natural standard which cannot simply be ignored or forgotten.

The natural scarcity of fuels can be understood through an analysis of (1) world energy balances, (2) reactivity with air and (3) energy density. World energy balances mirror crustal abundance for the elements. The International Energy Agency, British Petroleum, and the World Energy Council publish complimentary data sets on the physical abundance of available fuel resources and known reserves. For example, we know that existing *in situ* reserves for natural gas are far greater than those of crude oil. Reactivity with air denotes the rate at which a fuel will diminish, evaporate, or lose its embodied energy density. Crude oil begins to evaporate as it reacts with air; the best method to slow down this inevitable evaporation is to store crude oil in salt caverns, a process which demands seven barrels of water for every one barrel of stored crude. Finally, fuels possess an intrinsic energy density which is similar to that of foods. The energy density of fuels is measured in BTUs rather than calories. In the table below, we present this metric as it applies to various fuels.

FIG. 3: THE AVERAGE ENERGY
DENSITY OF VARIOUS ENERGY FUELS[34]

ENERGY FUEL TYPE	ENERGY DENSITY IN BRITISH THERMAL UNITS (BTU) PER KILOGRAM
Natural gas	53,570
Crude oil	41,846
Bituminous coal	20,871
Wood (dry)	15,555
Lignite (brown coal)	13,000
Peat	9,000

Different types of fuels provide an economy with varying potentialities for causing motion, work, or heat. Peat is less energy dense than natural gas. Crude oil is more energy dense than bituminous coal. By consequence, a given weight of crude oil will always produce more energy than an identical weight of coal or dry wood.

There are other factors which can be considered when analyzing the natural scarcity of fuels. These include: the time and energy embodiments required to explore, extract, transport, and store each kind of fuel, the long-term environmental sustainability and impact associated with the extraction and use of different fuels, and the ease of access to fuels located near population centres.

Our brief encounter here is meant to demonstrate that natural scarcity extends beyond the pure elements to the elemental compounds of foods and fuels.

APPENDIX II

We can never truly know when certain activities began, for some of our most cherished practices, customs, and innovations appear to have been practised since prehistoric times. We cannot accurately date inventions such as writing, shipbuilding, the wheel, and the plough. Likewise, no one can know with certainty when gold, silver, and copper were first mined and refined by humans. The most treasured antiquities of old, from ancient Egypt to ancient Greece, from ancient Iran to ancient India, show us that these civilizations not only had access to the rare metals of the earth, but also that they possessed a masterful *technê* in their ability to craft these metals into stunning artefacts.[35] The use of elemental metals for various purposes within ancient civilizations demonstrates a basic knowledge of the existence, nature, and qualities of these elements, as we see in the following table:

FIG. 4 THE KNOWLEDGE AND UTILIZATION OF THE
ELEMENTS IN ANCIENT WORLD CIVILIZATIONS UP TO
AND INCLUDING THE ROMAN EMPIRE[36]

ELEMENT NAME	REGIONS AND CIVILIZATIONS WITH A DEMONSTRATED USAGE	FORMS OF UTILIZATION
Gold	The Americas (Maya and other pre-Columbian civilizations in Central America and South America), Africa (Egyptians and Ethiopians), Middle East, Asia Minor, Mesopotamia, Akkad, Persia, Asia (including China), the Indus Valley, the Mediterranean (Etruscans, Greeks, and Romans), and Europe	Works of art and ornamentation; money and other financial instruments; medicine; pigmentation; articles for religious and ceremonial usage; thread and textiles; alloying; vessels; jewellery
Silver	The Americas, Africa (Egyptians), the Middle East, Asia Minor, Mesopotamia, Akkad, Persia, Asia (including China), the Indus Valley, the Mediterranean (Etruscans, Greeks, and Romans), and Europe	Works of art and ornamentation; money and other financial instruments; medicine; pigmentation; articles for religious and ceremonial usage; thread and textiles; alloying; vessels; jewellery; tools, implements and utensils
Lead	Africa (Egyptians), the Middle East and Asia Minor, Babylon, Anatolia, Persia, Asia (including China), the Indus Valley, the Mediterranean (Etruscans, Greeks, and Romans), and Europe	Alloying; medicine; alchemy (chemistry); pipes and plumbing; works of art and ornamentation; viticulture; paint; tools, implements and utensils; religious and ceremonial objects

Tin	The Americas, Africa (Egyptians), the Middle East, Asia Minor, Phoenicia, Phrygia, Anatolia, Persia, Asia (including China) the Indus Valley, the Mediterranean (Greeks and Romans) and Europe	Alloying (including the production of bronze); works of art and ornamentation; tools, implements, and utensils; vessels
Copper	Africa (Egyptians), the Middle East, Asia Minor, Asia (including China), the Indus Valley, the Mediterranean (Etruscans, Greeks, and Romans), and Europe	Tools, implements and utensils (including balance scales); works of art and ornamentation; architecture (including roofing); sheet metal and foil; wire; mirrors; hardware; cookware; jewellery; weapons; razors; cosmetics; plumbing; bells; pumps; valves; alloying; vessels; agriculture; money
Zinc	Africa (Egyptians), the Middle East, Asia Minor, Asia (including China), the Indus Valley, the Mediterranean (Greeks and Romans), and Europe	Alloying (especially in the production of brass); sheet metal; medicine; vessels; works of art and ornamentation; jewellery
Iron	The Americas, Africa (Egyptians), the Middle East, Asia Minor, Anatolia, Persia, Asia (including China), the Indus Valley, the Mediterranean (Greeks and Romans), and Europe	Tools, implements, and utensils; vessels; weapons; hardware; plumbing; religious and ceremonial objects

Similarly, the oldest written records that we have of human civilization, including those which cannot be perfectly dated, depict a world already rich in the sophisticated use of gold and silver as money. We will critically examine two important examples of these written records: the Hebrew Bible and the Codes of Ur-Nammu and Hammurabi. These texts will serve as historical case studies which attest to the seemingly perennial presence of the natural order of money.

THE HEBREW BIBLE

In the Book of Genesis, we are told that the first head of the river flowing out of the Garden of Eden went to Havilah, "where there is gold; and the gold in that land is good."[37] From this point onwards, the prophets repeatedly invoke gold, the practice of weighing gold, and the exchange of these weights of gold in their depictions of Israelite civilization throughout the ages. For example, we read that Abraham's servant presented Isaac's bride Rebekah with "a gold nose-ring weighing a half shekel, and two bracelets for her arms weighing ten gold shekels."[38] From this short passage, we can infer that the weight of gold in personal ornaments correlated directly to that gold's monetary value. In this sense, jewellery in the ancient world was far more than mere ornament—it was wearable estate. Likewise, any object made of pure gold or pure silver was not valued merely for its religious or artistic significance, but also for its status as money.

This idea is reinforced in the Book of Exodus, when the Israelites, upon being released from their enslavement in Egypt, are encouraged by God to acquire their due pay for their labour by taking the gold and silver jewellery of the Egyptian women.[39]

The emphasis on objective measurement in the form of tangibility and weight throughout the Hebrew Bible demonstrates the genuine sophistication of ancient Israel's monetary standard. Many examples attest to the use of gold for personal exchange and economic trans-actions. For example: when Abraham wishes to buy a field from Ephron, he is informed that the price is "four hundred shekels of silver". Abraham then "weighed out for Ephron the silver that he had named in the hearing of the Hittites, four hundred shekels of silver, according to the weights current among the merchants."[40] Later on, the prophet Isaiah alludes to this same practice of objective measurement when he describes "those who lavish gold from the purse, and weigh out silver in the scales."[41] Simi-larly, the prophet Jeremiah recounts that "I bought the field at Anathoth from my cousin Hanamel, and weighed out the money to him, seventeen shekels of silver. I signed the deed, sealed it, got witnesses, and weighed the money on scales."[42]

In all of these examples, we see that money is under-stood to be a standard weight of precious metal; it is not a coin whose substance is arbitrary, nor is it an abstract concept represented by an incidental instrument. It is for this reason that we see a consistent emphasis on weight and the act of weighing throughout the Hebrew Bible.

The importance of money as a standard weight of metal is even given moral significance, when God commands in the Book of Leviticus: "You shall not cheat in measuring length, weight, or quantity. You shall have honest balances, honest weights, an honest ephah, and an honest hin."[43] In the Book of Deuteronomy, God also proclaims: "You shall not have in your bag two kinds of weights, large and small. You shall not have in your house two kinds of measures, large and small. You shall have only a full and honest weight; you shall have only a full and honest measure, so that your days may be long in the land that the Lord your God is giving you."[44] Here, in the divine laws that define the very standards by which the Abrahamic community was to hold itself, we see the unwavering emphasis on the equitability of a natural standard of measurement—a standard which ought not to be cheated. This implies the broad diffusion as well as the prevalence of precious metal money within the community.

Complementing the passages which demonstrate the use of precious metals and the moral requirement that they be equitably measured, the Hebrew Bible also refers to their natural superiority over other ephemeral products of human cooperation. This is hinted in the descriptions of the Tent of Meeting and of the later Temple built by King Solomon, in which the most holy parts of these buildings required a large amount of pure gold as the only suitable metal for their construction.[45] Likewise, in prophesying the coming of the Messiah, the prophet Isaiah writes: "Instead of bronze I will bring gold, instead of iron I will bring silver; instead of wood, bronze, instead of stones, iron."[46] Here we see evidence of a sophisticated understanding of the natural order of money corresponding to each of the energy embodiments referenced in this passage. Isaiah orders the embodiments hierarchically, beginning with gold, the rarest of the four metals mentioned, and ending with iron, the most abundant; in each grouping, he recognizes that the higher-ranking embodiment renders it worthy of presentation to the Messiah over its lesser counterparts.

In the Book of Wisdom, Solomon observes that "Thou hast ordered all things in measure, number, and weight."[47] Commenting on this passage early in the fifth century AD, Saint Augustine of Hippo interprets this to mean that "measure fixes the mode of everything, number gives it its species, and weight gives it rest and stability."[48] The Hebraic understanding of the natural world, illuminated here by Saint Augustine, is one in which the corporeal, extended world (and the elements of which it is composed) is intrinsically ordered according to this threefold schema of material creation. Ultimately, the monetary systems of the Israelite civilization fit within this universal picture of the natural world. In other words, money itself adheres to the qualities which the whole of corporeal reality exhibits: money must be capable of being measured, numbered, and weighed.

For the ancient Israelites, there are underlying dynamics of nature, from the realities of the created world to the moral exhortations of God, which enforce the necessary use of precious metal money throughout time and across place. Money, therefore, is not a man-made addition to the natural world, but rather, the former emerges from and is supported by the latter. In these excerpts, we see the sophistication of the monetary system present in ancient Israel from Abraham to the later prophets. This exposition reveals that the natural order of money was comprehended and already in place long before the implementation of monetary instruments (such as the Lydian coins minted by King Croesus). Before the introduction of such instruments, money was understood simply to be a weight of gold and silver.

THE CODES OF UR-NAMMU
AND HAMMURABI

Historians generally agree that the earliest verifiable examples of human writing can be dated to the second or third millennium BC, in the ancient civilizations of Mesopotamia, Egypt, and the Indus Valley. For the purpose of our inquiry, the most relevant examples originate from Mesopotamia, a historic region situated between the Tigris and Euphrates rivers. In this part of the world, which is currently occupied by Iraq, the Sumerian, and Babylonian empires recorded agreements, events and law codes on clay tablets in cuneiform, a logo-syllabic script of wedge-shaped marks. We shall review two legal codes that have been preserved from this era: The Code of Ur-Nammu (c. 2100-2050 BC) and the Code of Hammurabi (c. 1755-1750 BC). Both codes were discovered and decoded in the 20th century. In these writings, we are provided with an invaluable opportunity to learn about the dynamics of human cooperation in these ancient societies. Let us begin with the Code of Ur-Nammu, which reads:

When the gods An and Elil turned over the kingship of the city of Ur to the god Nanna, at that time, for Ur-Namma, son born of the goddess Ninsun, for her beloved house-born slave, according to his justice and truth... gave to him

At that time, the nisku-people had control of the fields, the sea-captains had control of the foreign maritime trade... those who appropriate [the oxen]... those who appropriate [the sheep...]

[At that time, (I)], Ur-Namma, [mighty warrior, lord of the city of Ur, king of the lands of Sumer] and Akkad, [by the might] of the god Nanna, my lord, [by the true command of the God Utu], I established [justice in the land].

I returned. I established freedom for the Akkadians and foreigners in the lands of Sumer and Akkad, for those conducting foreign maritime trade (free from) the sea-captains, for the herdsmen (free from) those who appropriate oxen, sheep, and donkeys.

I made the copper bariga-measure and stand-ardized it at 60 silas. I made the cooper seah-measure, and standardized it at 10 silas. I made the normal king's copper seah-measure, and standardized it at 5 silas. I standardized (all) the stone weights (from) the pure 1-shekel weight to the 1-mina weight. I made the bronze 1-sila measure and standardized it at 1 mina.

I did not deliver the orphan to the rich. I did not deliver the widow to the mighty. I did not deliver the man with but one shekel to the man with one mina. I did not deliver the man with but one sheep to the man with one ox. I elim-inated enmity, violence, and cries for justice. I established justice in the land.[49]

In this excerpt, we see an appeal to freedom and egali-tarianism with Ur-Nammu's declaration that he is divinely entrusted to bestow the values of equity and truth for his people. A long string of assertions of power and authority concludes with the declaration that Ur-Nammu "established justice in the land", implying that, under the jurisdiction of the code, the purpose of his strength was to foster equity and objectivity, which we may understand as the wellspring of freedom in the egalitarian sense. Prosperity goes hand-in-hand with stability, and the combination of social stability manifest in Ur-Nammu's emphasis on equity is amplified by his proscription of "enmity" and "violence", thereby estab-lishing a means towards political stability as well.

We note the recurrence of weight and volume as objective forms of measurement throughout the code. This implies collective knowledge of the natural standard of measure and reward, as well as the insuperable role which it plays in the production, consumption, and exchange of energy embodiments. Ur-Nammu appeals to the naturally given standard by codifying into law measures of weight and volume in order to promote honest exchanges of energy embodiments within the economy. In the final statement of the code, Ur-Nammu declares: "I did not deliver the orphan to the rich. I did not deliver the widow to the mighty. I did not deliver the man with but one shekel to the man with one mina. I did not deliver the man with but one sheep to the man with one ox." Ur-Nammu clearly recognizes the need to inspire equitable cooperation among diverse people irrespective of their social position or relative wealth. In summary, the short code of Ur-Nammu provides us with important evidence of an ancient civilization that intuitively understood the natural order, its objective standard of measure and reward, and perhaps, with the final assertion, even ecological accountability.

The Code of Hammurabi echoes the virtues of Ur-Nammu's precedent code. Because this code is much longer, we shall be focusing on specific passages that are relevant to our inquiry. King Hammurabi repeatedly refers to the use of a standardized weight of gold and silver both in settling transactions and in rectifying a range of injustices between individuals. The standard *mina* and *shekel* weights are employed for lawful transactions and as restitution for false promises or broken contracts. A weight of silver is prescribed as appropriate compensation for bodily harm: "If one knock out a tooth of a freeman, he shall pay one-third mina of silver."[50] Similarly, if any instance of theft results in the loss of life, the local government must pay a weight of silver to the victim's family: "If it be a life (that is lost), the city and governor shall pay one mina of silver to his heirs."[51] Silver is also used as recompense for crimes that impact the natural productivity of the land: "If a man cut down a tree in a man's orchard, without the consent of the owner of the orchard, he shall pay one-half mina of silver."[52]

The Code of Hammurabi also contains multiple references evidencing personal use and cooperative exchanges of precious metals. We can see that there are specific legal obligations for any person entrusted with the transportation of precious metals: "If a man be on a journey and he give silver, gold, stones or portable property to a man with a commission for transportation, and if that man do not deliver that which was to be transported where it was to be transported, but take it to himself, the owner of the transported goods shall call that man to account for the goods to be transported which he did not deliver, and that man shall deliver to the owner of the transported goods fivefold the amount which was given to him."[53] This theme of regulating the fiduciary responsibilities pertaining to the custody of precious metals is repeated in two additional passages. For example: "If a man give to another silver, gold or anything else on deposit, whatever he gives shall show to witnesses and he shall arrange the

74

contracts and (then) he shall make the deposit."[54] And: "If a man give to another silver, gold or anything else on deposit in the presence of witnesses and the latter dispute with him (or deny it), they shall call that man to account and he shall double whatever he has disputed and repay it."[55] These statements are important because they illustrate sophisticated banking and investment activity using precious metal money.

The Code of Hammurabi reveals a complex precious metals monetary system wherein gold and silver were employed in savings, commerce and investment. Ultimately, the natural standard of measure and reward is extended to all members of society by virtue of precious metal money, thereby introducing a shared means by which equitable cooperation can be realized within and throughout the economic system.

SUMMARY OF FINDINGS

The objective of this historical study was to identify the oldest extant records of the monetary customs of human societies in order to establish when the practice of using precious metal money began. In pursuing this aim, we have uncovered a natural mystery worthy of amazement: the earliest records of written laws repeatedly refer to the use of fixed weights of silver and gold as money. We see within the context of these legal codes that an objective monetary standard served the purpose of fostering order, advancing egalitarianism, incentivizing dutiful and lawful behaviour, and promoting justice. Curiously, this complex set of cultural values, cooperative practices, and legal maxims appear already to be well established at the time of their writing.

In analyzing these ancient texts, we are presented with a range of compelling evidence that a gold and silver monetary standard has existed for thousands of years, with objectively dated law codes demonstrating the proliferation of such systems at least 4,100 years ago, and with the Hebrew Bible suggesting that these customs and practices are perhaps even more ancient than, or at least coeval with, the law codes of the Sumerian and Babylonian civilizations.

NOTES

1   Walt Whitman, "O Me! O Life!" in *Leaves of Grass* (Philadelphia: David McKay, 1892), p. 215.

2   Eccl. iii. 11 (New Revised Standard Version).

3   Cf. Saint Augustine, *Confessions* XI.

4   Because time is not measurable or equivalent to something physical, we resist the inclination of modern physics to identify time itself with the forces of energy and entropy.

5   For example, a calorie measures the amount of energy required to raise the temperature of a litre of water one degree Celsius at sea level. A British thermal unit (BTU) measures the intensity of heat required to raise one pound of water one degree Fahrenheit.

6   Water is essential as the medium or solvent in which these reactions take place, moving oxygen, nutrients, hormones and antibodies throughout the body. We group water within the category of foods because of its indispensable function in the metabolization of energy within the living body.

7   There is a tradition of historical thinkers who have similarly identified the importance of energy embodiments within the cooperative system and have correspondingly appreciated the distinction between the labourers that produce energy embodiments within an economy and those who do not. François Quesnay, Anne Robert Jacques Turgot, Thomas

Malthus, Karl Marx, and Sergei Podolinsky have all proposed economic theories of this type. Their theories tend to go too far in abstracting from the qualitative facts of nature by advancing mathematically calculable, theoretical systems that ostensibly predict all manner of economic activity (e.g., the project of the *tableau économique*; or the attempt to calculate the numerical value of energy input and energy output of an entire economy; or the labour theory of value; or the Malthusian food and population models). These theories can also appear tendentious insofar as they serve to justify the establishment of powerful central governments to command social, political, and economic reform. We define energy embodiments and understand their role in human cooperation philosophically; by consequence, we accept that all human cooperation is powered by the conservation and expenditure of energy embodiments. This observation elucidates the temporal energetic dependency of all economic participants upon the production, consumption, and exchange of these fundamental currencies of cooperation. At this stage, it would be an error to extrapolate from this observation anything more than the mere recognition of this dependency. This recognition will ultimately lead us towards our understanding of ecological accountability in the fifth chapter.

8   We will often substitute the male 'farmer' as the agent who stands for the whole host of real economic actors to which we refer.

9   These are not ethical judgements but principles of practical action given by the natural order as the real economy wrestles with it. With that being said, it may be profitable for other thinkers to conduct sociological or ethical explorations of these principles.

10 Although the categories of real economy and service economy are distinct, we fully acknowledge that some members in the service economy significantly contribute to the efficiency of the real economy without being farmers or miners themselves (e.g. the scientist who studies how to eradicate the boll weevil or increase the bee population; or the maker of the plough or combine or irrigation system). There are indeed occupations that are closer to the real economy and others that are further away. But the existence of this grey area does not itself disturb or vitiate the intelligibility of a categorical distinction.

11 A service economy that has forgotten ecological accountability must dominate (and historically has dominated) the real economy through physical force, psychological manipulation, and monetary debasement. In the past, physical force was the essential means of domination. The historical record of nearly every culture is thus tainted with barbarous acts of human slavery and reprehensible rules of tyranny. In recent times, physical force has generally been supplanted by psychological manipulation and monetary debasement. The most obvious consequence of all forms of domination is the consolidation and centralization of political and geographical power by members of the service economy. Consequently, the social, political, and economic policies carried out by governments can subordinate or completely disregard the temporal energetic dependency of all members upon the activity of the real economy. Put simply, all three methods of dominating the real economy are attempts to master rather than obey the natural order itself.

12 See William Stanley Jevons, *Money and the Mechanism of Exchange* (London: H.S. King & Company, 1876).

13 Ibid., II, p. 8.

14 Ibid., II, p. 11.

15 Ibid., II, p. 9.

16 We group academics following in the tradition of Adam Smith and John Maynard Keynes as expressing the position of the modern economist. We group academics following in the tradition of David Graeber as expressing the position of the modern anthropologist.

17 We have shown that everything which lives and moves must metabolize, or conserve and expend energy embodiments. This is an essential insight because it implies that subsistence, rather than overproduction, is the initial objective in any real economic activity. The real economy has the potential to produce the things it needs to consume—things that are useful such as food, energy, and basic materials. Put simply, the farmer's initial objective is to work so that he may live. The service economy, on the other hand, is always overproducing because it cannot subsist on its own products. Having ignored ecological accountability, the economist and anthropologist take the overproduction of energy embodiments for granted, as if it were the default state of cooperation. In this imaginary world where the products of the real economy are assumed to exist in a perpetual state of overproduction, the two schools then quarrel over *how* (exchange markets vs. altruism) and *why* (invisible hand vs. moral obligations) these energy embodiments move from the one segment of society to the other.

18 This insight may be extended to address commonly held economic myths about hoarding. If we hoard energy embodiments, "we will open our safe and find ashes". An expression taken from Annie Dillard's *The Writing Life* (New York: Harper-Perennial, 1990), pp. 78-79.

19 In more recent times, economists have argued that peculiar

historical examples such as wampum shells, cowry shells, or variously shaped stones and paper show that money does not necessarily need to be useful. We object by challenging economists to expand their geographic scope of observation over the same time period. They shall always find that elsewhere a useful energy embodiment is employed as money, often by a more productive or complex society. This contextualizes the claim to history on the part of economists, as their examples often depict rare monetary experiments which have, in every instance, failed or disappeared. The economist might respond to our objection by pointing to our modern era, when the great majority of nations employ a contrived money that is not an energy embodiment. If history is any guide, these instances, however ubiquitous now, will in time become failed monetary experiments and disappear like their predecessors. Our belief is supported by the fact that, even in our present age, governments and central banks continue to settle their own trading activities and transactions with energy embodiments, including crude oil, natural gas, gold, copper, grain, etc. One might even go so far as arguing that even in our own era, useful energy embodiments serve as money between the rich and those in power when they trade amongst their peers while a double standard compels the common citizen to be measured and rewarded by moneys that have no independent use.

20 Diamonds and gems would be inferior moneys for they are neither homogeneous nor mutually interchangeable.

21 See Eric R. Scerri, *The Periodic Table: Its Story and Significance* (Oxford: Oxford University Press, 2006).

22 In our inquiry, we shall exclude the 30 elements which are either generated in a laboratory or exist in extreme trace quantities.

23   See Appendix I for our further reflections on the natural scarcity of foods and fuels.

24   Silver does not react with oxygen or water but it does discolour when exposed to sulfur-containing substances. This is called tarnishing and can be easily removed; it is different from rusting or corrosion, which destroys metals such as iron when they react with oxygen.

25   Michael John Bloomfield and Roy Maconachie, *Gold* (Cambridge: Polity Press, 2021), p. 6

26   See W.M. Haynes, *CRC Handbook of Chemistry and Physics 97th Edition* (CRC Press, 2016). The Mohs scale of mineral hardness was introduced in 1822 by Friedrich Mohs in his *Treatise on Mineralogy*.

27   See Appendix II for a historical investigation into the earliest use of precious metal money.

28   The word 'champaign' is being employed here to denote flat, open country and not the US town or the sparkling wine.

29   Hans Christoph Binswanger argues that by the end of the Middle Ages, political leaders came to realize that alchemy would never succeed in transmuting base metals into gold, and so the project of wealth creation *ex nihilo* gradually shifted from alchemists to economists. See Hans Christoph Binswanger, *Money and Magic: A Critique of Modern Economy in Light of Goethe's Faust* (Chicago: University of Chicago Press, 1994).

30   We define money as an energy embodiment that reflects ecological accountability by inviting all members to cooperate in accordance with the natural standard of measure and reward. It is important to stress once more that, in a post-subsistence society, we very much see the real and service economies as symbiotic. We have no difficulty in accepting that individuals in the service economy may succeed far and

above individuals in the real economy without having tilled the earth or mined for ore. It would be a methodological error and indeed an impossibility to fully calculate or fully predict these outcomes. Our chief concern is that society as a whole be guided by ecological accountability at all times.

31 There are further considerations to be taken into account when farming: fertilizer and pesticide usage, climate, richness of soil, season, atmospheric conditions, and potential for disease. The crop yield data in our table assumes that a crop is being cultivated within an accommodative environment using general practices.

32 Hannah Ritchie and Max Roser, *Crop Yields* (Our World in Data, 2018).

33 Cantwell, M. and T. Suslow. 2002, Produce Fact Sheet, UC Davis, http://postharvest.ucdavis.edu/Commodity_Resources/Fact_ Sheets/ (Accessed July 2022).

34 This table was prepared by Stefan Wieler CFA, CAIA the former VP of Research at Goldmoney Inc. with information sourced from the US Energy Information Administration (EIA).

35 As will be revealed by any visit to the British Museum, the Louvre, the Metropolitan Museum of Art, the Museum of Egyptian Antiquities, the Israel Museum in Jerusalem, the Benaki Museum, the Hermitage Museum, the National Archeological Museum in Athens, the Aachen Cathedral Treasury, the Capitoline Museums, the Istanbul Archaeological Museums, and many others.

36 This table is the product of both original research and drawing upon the following works, *inter alia*: Theophrastus, *On Stones*, translated by John F. Richards (Columbus, Oh.: Ohio State University, 1956); Raymond C. Moore, *Introduction to Historical Geology* (New York: Mc-Graw-Hill Book Co.,

1949); J.C. Yannopoulos, *The Extractive Metallurgy of Gold* (New York: Van Nostrand Reinhold, 1991); George Louis Leclerc, *Natural History, abridged: including the history of the elements, the earth, mountains, insects & vegetables* (London: C. & G. Kearsley, 1792); Hugh Aldersey-Williams, *Periodic Tales: a cultural history of the elements, from arsenic to zinc* (New York: Ecco, 2011).

37   Gen. ii. 11-12.

38   Gen. xxiv. 22 (King James Version).

39   Exod. iii. 22; xi. 2; xii. 35 (New Revised Standard Version).

40   Gen. xxiii. 15-16.

41   Isa. xlvi. 6.

42   Jer. xxxii. 9-10.

43   Lev. xix. 35-37.

44   Deut. xxv. 13-16.

45   See Exod. xxv-xxviii; I Kings vi. 19-31.

46   Isa. lx. 17.

47   Wis. xi. 20 (King James Version).

48   Saint Augustine, *De Gen. ad Litt.* (New York: New City Press, 1999), IV. 7.

49   H.A. Hoffner and M.T. Roth, *Law Collections from Mesopotamia and Asia Minor* (Atlanta: Scholars Press, 1997), 15-17.

50   R.F. Harper, *The Code of Hammurabi* (Chicago: The University of Chicago Press, 1904), §201.

51   Harper (1904), §24.

52   Harper (1904), §59.

53   Harper (1904), §112.

54   Harper (1904), §122.

55   Harper (1904), §124.

INDEX

access: to fuels, 61; to rare metals, 63
accountability: ecological (*See* ecological
    accountability); intra-personal,
    man-made standard promoting, 36;
    to natural standard of measure and
    reward, 23–24; to other economic
    members in relation to natural world,
    31; of the real economy, 32; of service
    economy to real economy, 24
action, reality of time for, 8
aggregate demand, 29
air, reactivity with. *See* reactivity with air
alchemy, 54, 82n29
altruism, 80n17
aluminum, 42
analysis, 3
animals, metabolism in, 11
antimicrobial elements, 46
Augustine of Hippo, Saint, 69
axiomatic formulations, 3

beryllium, 42
Binswanger, Hans Christoph, 82n29
biological metabolism, 11
bismuth, 42
Book of Deuteronomy, 68
Book of Ecclesiastes, 6
Book of Exodus, 67
Book of Genesis, 66
Book of Leviticus, 68
Book of Wisdom, 69
British Petroleum, 60
brittle solids, 42–43

calcium, 44
caloric embodiment of foods, 58, 77n5

Carlyle, Thomas, 3
chain of temporal energy dependency,
    16–17
Code of Hammurabi, 70–71, 73–76
Code of Ur-Nammu, 70–73, 75–76
collective system: cooperation between
    diverse activities in, 1–2 (*See also*
    cooperative system[s]); real and
    sustainable prosperity for, 2
compound elements, 57. *See also*
    food(s); fuels
conductivity, 45–46
conservation, as guiding principle of
    cooperation, 29
conservation of energy, 10–12: from food,
    20–21; in human activity, 15
consumption: around present system, 54;
    of energy embodiments, 15, 16, 31 (*See
    also* food[s]; fuels); in parasitic systems,
    29; in real economy, 20–22; in service
    economy, 19–22, 26
contrived moneys, 51–53, 81n10
cooperation: collective desire for,
    36; between diverse activities, 1–2;
    ecological accountability as underlying
    and guiding principle of, 27, 28;
    energy embodiments as fundamental
    currencies of, 18, 31; with environment,
    16; generated products of, 8; key
    principles of, 31; man-made standard
    promoting, 36; money as common
    measure and reward of, 33–34;
    in parasitic systems, 29; between
    persons and ecological environment,
    3; sustainable, 36, 55; unsustainable
    forms of, 51–52

85

cooperative system(s), 15–24: actions allowed in, 8; energy-dense foods in, 59; energy embodiments in, 18–19, 37, 77–78n7; and natural order, 26; negotiation between man and nature in, 50; primary cooperators with nature in, 17–18; real and service economies in, 19–20; real economy as, 22–24; relation of nature and society as, 3; as thermodynamic systems, 15

copper: ancient civilizations' use of, 63, 65; antimicrobial properties of, 46; conductivity of, 45–46; crustal abundance of, 44; malleability of, 42; melting point of, 45; reactivity with air, 43

crop yields, 57–59, 83n31

crustal abundance: crop yields vs., 57; of precious elements, 47; of pure elements, 43–45; and world energy balances, 60

currencies of cooperation, energy embodiments as, 18, 31, 33

degeneration: cycle of generation and, 9–10, 31, 50, 51; in parasitic systems, 29; in real economy, 22

dependence: chain of temporal energy dependency, 16–17; of cooperative systems on natural order, 26; of economies on natural order (*See* ecological accountability); interdependence of energy and entropy, 9–10; on nature, for energy embodiments, 26–27; of real economy on natural order, 26; of service economy on natural order, 25, 26; of service economy on real economy, 20, 25; of society on natural world, 51

diamonds, as money, 81n20

difficulty in obtaining energy embodiments, 39–40, 42–46

directionality, of time's movement, 6–7

"dismal science," 2–3

ductile solids, 42, 47

ecological accountability, 25–30: circle of, 27–28; current unfamiliarity with, 52–53; definition of, 25–26; divorce of economic activity from, 29; gold money as mirror of, 49–55; as limit on human desires, 35; money as mirror of, 32, 54–55; and natural scarcity of foods, 59; as respect for nature's limits and edicts, 32; responsibility for, 29–32; as underlying and guiding principle of all cooperation and sustainable prosperity, 27, 28, 31–32, 51

ecological environment, cooperation between persons and, 3. *See also* natural world

economics: and condition of temporality, 7–8; intersection of nature and human intention in, 3; natural philosophy method of, 3–4; theories of (*See* economic theories)

economic systems: in circle of ecological accountability, 27–28; in context of time, 8; energy embodiments as currencies of cooperation in, 18, 31; food producers in, 16–18; fuel producers in, 17–18; parasitic, 28–29; primary materials producers in, 17–18; responsibility for ecological accountability in, 29–32; surplus of food for persistence of, 16

economic terms, x–xi

economic theories, 77–78n7: current, 2–3; definitions of money in, 34; methodologies of, 2; unsustainable forms of cooperation in, 51–52

economy(-ies): broken into parts, 3; physical expression of energy and entropy at individual level of, 15; real (*See* real economy); service (*See* service economy)

electrical conductivity, 45–46

elemental producers, 17–18

elements/elemental substances. *See also specific elements*: compound, 57–61; early mining, refining, and uses of, 63–65; as energy embodiments, 12–13, 33; as energy source, 12–13; as money, 42–46, 66–76 (*See also* natural order of money); natural scarcity of, 41–42, 57–61; precious metals, 43, 46–48 (*See also* precious metals); pure (*See* pure elements); qualities and potentialities of, 41; states of, 42–44, 47; that occur naturally on earth, 41

employment: abstract, 51–52; in real vs. in service economies, 52

energy, 9–13: conservation of, 10–12, 15, 20–21; definition of, 10; expending of, 11–12, 15, 20–21; as generative force in nature, 9; interdependence of entropy and, 9–10; metabolism as thermodynamic processes which conserve and expend, 11–12; required to extract elements from nature, 44; as source of life, movement, activity, and heat, 11 (*See also* food[s]; fuels); thermodynamic law of entropy and, 10–13, 15

energy density: of foods, 57–59; of fuels, 59–61

energy dependency, temporal, 16–17

energy embodiments, 12–13. *See also specific types of embodiments*: in circle of ecological accountability, 27–28; in cooperative systems, 77–78n7; as currencies of cooperation, 18; definition of, 18–19; dependence on generation of, 26–27, 50, 51; for extracting elements from nature, 44; for fuel production/storage, 61; hoarding of, 80n18; Isaiah's ordering of, 69; as measures and rewards, 33–34, 37; as money, 37–38, 81n10 (*See also* natural order of money); money as, 33–38; in the natural order, 13; natural pulse of, 32; natural scarcity of, 57–61;

natural standard of measure and reward in exchange of, 73 (*See also* natural standard of measure and reward); in real economy, 19–22, 33–34; in service economy, 19–22

energy sources. *See also specific sources*: foods, 57–59; fuels, 59–61; non-biological and biological, 12; primary materials/elemental substances, 12–13

entropy, 9–10; resistance to, 40, 42–47; thermodynamic law of energy and, 10–13, 15

exchange: of energy embodiments, natural standard of measure and reward in, 73; money as mechanism of, 34–35; of precious metals, 74–75; of products of human action, 31

exchange markets, 80n17

exports, 52

false moneys, 52–53

food(s): as biological sources of energy, 12; as compounds of elements, 57; conservation of energy from, 20–21; and cooperation between man and environment, 15; crop yields, 57–59, 83n31; effects of entropy on, 40; elemental substances in harvesting of, 12–13; energy density of, 57–59; expending energy from, 15, 20–21; natural scarcity of, 57–59; primary producers of, 16–18; storage life after harvest of, 57–59; time from sowing to harvest for, 57–59; water as, 77n6

food producers, 16–18, 59, 78n8

French Revolution, 29

frugality, ideal of, 24

fuel producers, 17–18

fuels: as compounds of elements, 57; effects of entropy on, 40; elemental substances in harvesting of, 12–13; energy density of, 59–61;

fuels, *continued*
as energy embodiments, 33; natural
scarcity of, 59–61; as non-biological
sources of energy, 12; primary
cooperators with nature in production
of, 17, 18; reactivity with air by, 59, 60;
world energy balances of, 59–60
the future, 6

gases, 42
gems, as money, 81n20
generation: cycle of degeneration and,
9–10, 31, 50, 51; in parasitic systems, 29;
in real economy, 22
gold, 49–50: ancient civilizations' use of,
63, 64, 66; antimicrobial properties of,
46; attributes of, 47, 48; conductivity
of, 45, 46; crustal abundance of, 44,
47; as ductile solid, 42; malleability of,
42; as money, 66 (*See also* gold money);
in natural order of money, 48, 54–55;
weight of, 45, 47; when exposed to air, 43
gold money, 48–49: and contrived moneys,
51–53; historical examples of, 66–70,
73–76; intrinsic limitations of natural
order reflected by, 50; as measure and
reward, 50; as mirror of ecological
accountability, 49–55
Graeber, David, 80n16
Great Depression, 29
gross domestic product, 29

Hammurabi, King, 73
Hebrew Bible, 66–70, 75–76
historical monetary systems, 66–76: Code
of Hammurabi, 70–71, 73–76; Code of
Ur-Nammu, 70–73, 75–76; in Hebrew
Bible, 66–70, 75–76
hoarding, 80n18
human activities: dating of, 63; energy
embodiments of, 18, 20–21; energy
expended in, 15; money as measure and

reward of, 32, 33; natural vs. service,
1–2; of primary cooperators with
nature, 17–18; products of (*See* products
of human action); in real economy,
19–21; in service economy, 19, 21;
within time, 7–8
human intention, intersection of nature
and, 3
human lives, underlying dynamic of, 15
humans: aging in, 5; food needed by, 12;
key principles of cooperation among, 31
(*See also* cooperative system[s]); metabolism
in, 11; sense of passage of time in, 6;
sustainable prosperity for, 30; sustainable
relationship between nature and, 28
human systems, construction and
resilience of, 9

ideals, to prosper in natural world, 24, 32
ideation, 24
imports, 52
inequity, in parasitic economy, 29
International Energy Agency, 60
invisible hand, 80n17
iron: ancient civilizations' use of, 65;
reactivity with air of, 43
irreversibility of time, 6–7, 13
Isaiah, xiii, 68–69
Israel, ancient, 66–70, 75–76

Jevons, William Stanley, 34–35

Keynes, John Maynard, 80n16

labour theory of value, 78n7
laws of nature: thermodynamic law of
energy and entropy, 10–13; time, 6
lead: ancient civilizations' use of, 64;
crustal abundance of, 44; as ductile
solid, 42; malleability of, 42
legal codes: Code of Hammurabi, 70–71,
73–76; Code of Ur-Nammu, 70–73, 75–76

limits: on human desires, placed by ecological accountability, 35; intrinsic, of natural order, 50

liquids, 42

machines, elemental substances as energy sources for, 13

malleability, 42

Malthusian food and population models, 78n7

Malthus, Thomas, 78n7

Marx, Karl, 78n7

matter: changes in, 10; states of, 42–44, 47; thermodynamic flow of energy through, 13

measure(s): delusive, 29; energy embodiments as, 33–34, 37; gold money as, 50; money as, 32–34; natural standard of, 22–24 (*See also* natural standard of measure and reward); of prosperity, 52; in real and service economies, 55; of the same kind as standards for real economy, 34; standard weights of metals, 67–68

mechanical metabolism, 12

melting point, 45, 47

mercury, 46

Mesopotamian civilization, 70–76

metabolism, 80n17: as all thermodynamic processes which conserve and expend energy, 11–12; biological, 11; mechanical, 12

monetary systems: historical examples of, 66–76, 80–81n19; sociological or anthropological features arising from adoption of, 36–37

monetary theory, ix–xi

money, 32–38: as concrete reflection of nature, 2; contrived, 51–53, 81n10; definitions of, 34–36, 82n30; diamonds or gems as, 81n20; economic nature, purpose, and role of, 32; as energy embodiment, 33–38; energy embodiments as, 37–38, 81n10; essence, purpose, and role of, 2, 32; false, 52–53; gold as, 66–70, 73–76 (*See also* gold money); historical terms used to define, 36; Jevons' definition of, 35; as mirror of ecological accountability, 32, 54–55; natural order of, 2 (*See also* natural order of money); philosophy of, ix–xi; pure elements as, 41–42, 66–76 (*See also individual elements*); silver as, 66–70, 73–76; as simultaneously measure and reward, 32–35; as social contract, 36–37; as subjective or relative, 37; time factor for, 39; triad of natural order, time, and, 5

Money and the Mechanism of Exchange (Jevons), 34–35

movement of time, 6–7

natural forms, 42

natural order, 1–4: accountability to, 24 (*See also* ecological accountability); cooperative systems' dependence on, 26; crustal abundance in, 44; definition of, 2; embodiments of energy within, 13; energy in, 9–13; generative cycles within, 29, 50, 51; gold as reflecting intrinsic limitations of, 50; limits prescribed by, 32; of money (*See* natural order of money); natural scarcity in, 40; real economy's dependence on, 25–26; service economy's secondary dependence on, 25, 26; standard of measure and reward in, 22–24 (*See also* natural standard of measure and reward); time in, 5–8

natural order of money, 5, 39–48: characteristics for, 39; in Code of Hammurabi, 70–71, 73–76; in Code of Ur-Nammu, 70–73, 75–76; definition of, 2, 47; gold in, 49, 54–55 (*See also* gold money); in Hebrew Bible, 66–70, 75–76; superior choice for, 39–40

natural philosophy, 3–4

natural scarcity, 40: applied to energy embodiments, 57–61; crustal abundance, 43–45; definition of, 41; of foods, 57–59; of fuels, 59–61; in generative and degenerative cycles, 51; and properties of solid elements, 44–45; of pure elements, 41–45; subjective desires of peripheral actors vs., 53–54

natural standard of measure and reward, 22–24: collective knowledge of, 73; definition of, 23; economic activity anchored to, 35–37, 49 (*See also* gold money); and exchange of energy embodiments, 73; money as reflection and extension of, 33–35 (*See also* natural order of money); money reflecting upper limit of, 40; and natural scarcity of foods, 59; objective scarcity in, 53–54; sustainable prosperity dependent on, 30

natural world: differing relationships with, 1; Hebraic understanding of, 69; ideals for prospering in, 24; irreducibility of, 3; qualitative facts in, 4; societies' dependence on, 51

nature: as concrete reflection of money, 2; continuous human interaction with, to survive, 15; extracting elements from, 44; and food production, 16–17; generative and degenerative cycles of, 9–10, 31; intersection of human intention and, 3; Israelites' understanding of underlying dynamics of, 69–70; laws of, 6, 10–13; limits and edicts of, 32; primary cooperators with, 17–18, 33; pure elements in, 41–42 (*See also* elements/ elemental substances); real economy cooperation with, 22–24; relation of cooperative society to, 3; sustainable relationship between humanity and, 28; as thermodynamic system, 9; of time, 6–7; time as superseding law of, 6

nickel, 44

nominal growth, 29
numerical data, 3

overproduction, 80n17
oxygen, 44

palladium: attributes of, 47; crustal abundance of, 47; when exposed to air, 43

parasitic economy, 53
parasitic systems, 28–29
the past, 6
philosophy: of money, ix–xi; natural, 3–4
platinum: attributes of, 47; crustal abundance of, 47; in natural order of money, 48; weight of, 47; when exposed to air, 43

Podolinsky, Sergei, 78n7
political stability, 72
post-subsistence, 22, 40
precious metals, 43, 46–47, 63. *See also individual metals*: first mining and refining of, 63; as money, historical study of, 66–76; in natural order of money, 48 (*See also* natural order of money); standard weight of, 67–68; use and exchange of, 74–75

the present, 6–8
preservation, ideal of, 24
prices, 52–53
primary cooperators with nature, 17–18, 33
primary materials. *See also* elements/ elemental substances: as energy embodiments, 33; as energy source, 12–13; primary cooperators with nature in production of, 17

products of human action: energy embodiments as, 18; exchange of, 31; expending energy as, 15; in real and service economies, 80n17

prosperity: delusive sense of, 28, 29; ideals for, 24, 32; measures of, 52; money